(The very wonderful, all true)

Wizard of Oz

Pictorial Book of Trivia

Featuring

Judy Garland as "Dorothy"

...

Rita E. Piro

The Very Wonderful, All True Wizard of Oz Pictorial Book of Trivia

featuring Judy Garland as Dorothy

Great Feats Press - New York

All images from The Classic Image Collection.

Manufactured in the United States of America

Library of Congress Data available upon request

ISBN 0-9706261-1-8

10 9 8 7 6 5 4 3 2

For more information, please visit us at oztriviabook.com or judygarland.net or e-mail

oztriviabook@aol.com

For my parents,

For Joseph, Gerald, Thomas and Susan,

Elisabeth, and Mark,

For David

and

For NM & RM

(The very wonderful, all true)

Wizard of Oz

Pictorial Book of Trivia

Featuring

Judy Garland as "Dorothy"

"It is almost sacred. I don't want anybody, anywhere to lose the thing they have about Dorothy and that song."

- Judy Garland explaining why she would never poke fun at The Wizard of Oz or "Over the Rainbow."

Left, L.Frank Baum, author of 'The Wonderful Wizard of Oz' and, bottom, the cast of the 1903 stage version of the book. This original stage version was immensely popular and ran for several years.

1

From the book by...

1. The 1939 film version of *The Wizard of Oz* was adapted from the children's fantasy book, *The Wonderful Wizard of Oz*.

2. *The Wonderful Wizard of Oz* was written by L. (Lyman) Frank Baum and illustrated by W.W. (William Wallace) Denslow. It was released in 1900.

3. There are forty separate books in the *Oz* series.

4. According to his family, L. Frank Baum came up with the name *Oz* after he looked at a file cabinet whose top drawer was marked "A-N" and bottom drawer, "O-Z"

5. L. Frank Baum adapted a stage version of *The Wizard of Oz* himself, one that was reworked by the producers of the show. The stage version featured Dorothy and her pet cow, Imogene, who were swallowed up by a twister and came to rest somewhere in the land of the Munchkins.

6. *The Wizard of Oz* in the above-described stage version premiered at the Majestic Theatre in New York City on January 20, 1903, with a cast that featured David Montgomery, Fred Stone, Anna Laughlin, Arthur Hill, Bessie Wynn, and Grace Kimball. It was a huge success, running several years.

7. The first screen version of *Oz* was handled by Baum himself in a 1908 production that combined live stage and on-screen elements. The production proved very expensive and did not succeed.

8. In 1914 Baum founded the "Oz Film Manufacturing Co." in Hollywood. The company produced five silent features and a few shorts based on Baum's *Oz* stories. The films were neither a critical or financial success, and the studio folded the following year in 1915.

9. Ruth Plumly Thompson took over the writing of the *Oz* series after the death of L. Frank Baum in 1919. Her first book was *The Royal Book of Oz*, published under Baum's name, but written by Plumly.

10. Baum's son, Frank Jayson Baum, who billed himself professionally as "L. Frank Baum, Jr.," supervised the licensing of his father's material after the elder Baum's death.

11. Although the newly-formed MGM studios tried to obtain the film rights to *The Wizard of Oz* in 1924, Baum, Jr. sold them to Chadwick Pictures, which released a silent film version of the story a year later.

12. The first silent film version of *Oz,* written by Baum, Jr., starred Oliver Hardy (just before he teamed up with Stan Laurel) as the Tin Woodsman.

13. The 1925 silent screen version of *Oz* did away with much of the familiar *Oz* story in favor of a story with strong romantic inclinations.

14. NBC produced a radio series version of *The Wizard of Oz* during the 1933-1934 broadcast season.

15. L. Frank Baum was born on May 15, 1856 in Chittenango, New York. Every year the town has a huge *Oz* celebration in his honor. Baum died on May 5, 1919 at his home in Hollywood.

Below, the 1925 silent film version of The Wizard of Oz starring Oliver Hardy as The Tin Man, Larry Semon as The Scarecrow and Dorothy Dwan as Dorothy.

Top, The MGM studio in 1928, bottom, the famed MGM main gate in 1943.

2

The Studio

1. *The Wizard of Oz* was produced as a technicolor film in 1939 by the Metro-Goldwyn-Mayer Studios, known popularly as Metro or MGM.

2. MGM was controlled by the Loew's Theatre Corporation, owners of the largest chain of movie theatres in the country. The Loew's corporate headquarters were located in New York City in offices above the State Theatre in Times Square at 43rd Street & Broadway. Loew's Corporation president was Nicholas Schenck.

3. Loew's had 125 theatres in the United States and Canada with twenty-six in the NYC area alone. All MGM movies were shown in Loew's theatres.

4. MGM was formed in 1924 through the merger of Louis B. Mayer Pictures, Samuel P. Goldwyn Pictures and Metro Pictures owned by Marcus Loew.

5. MGM was actually located in Culver City, California, not Hollywood. The lot was the original home of Triangle Studios.

6. The main lot of MGM was a city within a city, with its own police and fire departments, hospital, shops, telegraph and post offices.

7. By the late 1930's, there were a total of twenty-eight soundstages at MGM. Stage #15 was the largest in the world.

8. In 1939, MGM was the largest movie studio in the world and its top executive, Louis B. Mayer, was the highest paid salaried executive in the world with an annual income of 1.25 million dollars.

9. MGM first introduced its trademark, "Leo the Lion," in a 1928 silent movie. In the circular band framing Leo's head was the MGM motto: "*Ars Gratia Artis*" ("*Art For Art's Sake*")

10. There were two real live "Leo the Lions" which were kept in a compound on the studio lot.

11. The MGM slogan was, "More stars than there are in the heavens."

12. The MGM studio had an extraordinary commissary featuring many of Mama Mayer's recipes, the most famous of which were for matzoh ball and chicken noodle soups. (r. L.B. Mayer & his second wife.)

13. During its heyday in the 1930's and 1940's, the MGM studios produced an average of one film a week.

14. The regular work schedule was nine to six during the week and a possible half day on Saturday. During this time period, nearly all of American businesses also held to a half-day of work on Saturday.

15. The MGM Studio was sold in 1970 to Kirk Kerkorian, who auctioned off the studio's prized possessions, and sold 38 acres of the studio's back lots to housing developers. It is now owned by Sony Entertainment.

16. Ted Turner bought the MGM film library in 1986 and started to colorize many classics. Warner Brothers Studios recently purchased the MGM classic film library from Turner.

Top, L.B. Mayer at his desk in his grand, all-white office. Said partner, Sam Goldwyn, of Mayer's office: "You need an automobile to reach the desk."

Louis B. Mayer

A founding member of the Academy of Motion Picture Arts and Sciences, Louis B. Mayer was born Eliezer (Lazar) Meir in the Ukraine in 1885. His family emigrated to America, specifically Boston, the following year. Mayer was married in 1904 to Margaret Shenberg, a union that produced two daughters, Irene (married to producer David O. Selznick) and Edith. Mayer divorced his first wife in 1942 and married Lorena Danker in 1948.

After buying one movie theatre in 1907 and turning it into the largest theatre chain in New England, Mayer expanded into film distribution, making a half-million dollars from distributing the D.W. Griffith film, *Birth of a Nation*. He soon formed his own California film production company, Louis B. Mayer pictures.

After a series of mergers with Samuel Goldwyn Films and Metro Pictures, Mayer's production company became known as Metro-Goldwyn-Mayer Studios. It was under Louis B. Mayer's leadership that MGM became the biggest and most prestigious studio in Hollywood, turning out some of the world's most well-known and best-loved classic films and film stars.

There have been wildly contrasting characterizations of L.B. Mayer. Many have painted a portrait of the man as an overbearing, heartless, and cruel despot who exploited all those who worked for him.

Others, including Hollywood's Golden Age stars Van Johnson, Janet Leigh, Jane Powell, Margaret O'Brien and June Allyson, have consistently denied this one-sided take of the man, saying that while he was indeed a demanding and ruthless businessman, Mayer was far more of a caring, benevolent and supportive boss to the vast majority of his stars.

During Louis B. Mayer's tenure at MGM, the "studio system" reigned supreme. Under this system, actors and actresses were contract salaried workers, bound to perform in any capacity that the studio dictated. This included film roles, promotional appearances, radio shows and in advertising. Stars were also bound by strict morals clauses in their contracts.

Above all, Mayer was a fervent believer in an apple pie-America. He had changed his original birthday to coincide with that of the United States, (July 4), and annually held a huge birthday party for himself and his beloved adopted country at his beach home. Under Mayer's direction, MGM regularly produced films that underscored the importance of family, the wisdom of motherhood and the glory of the Stars and Stripes.

Between 1947 and 1954, the House Un-American Activities Committee (HUAC) became indirectly involved in the regulation of films. The HUAC members

"We called him 'Pops,' and he was so good to so many of us, really"

- Jane Powell on Louis B. Mayer

considered it their duty to purge the country of any Communist influences. During the initial hearings, so-called "friendly witnesses" were asked to testify. These people were not under suspicion and provided general statements concerning any knowledge they might have of any Communist activity in Hollywood. Louis B. Mayer and Jack Warner represented the studio heads at the hearings.

By 1950, America's taste in films had changed, giving way to an edgier portrayal of life, far darker than anything Louis B. Mayer had ever imagined would be seen - or that anyone would want to see - on film. Such emphasis on this new film genre, coupled with the burgeoning medium of television which cut sharply into movie theatre revenues, led to Mayer's ouster from MGM in 1951 and his replacement as head of production and development by his onetime assistant, Dory Schary.

Louis B. Mayer died in October 1957. In 1969, the Louis B. Mayer Library was founded by the American Film Institute and the faculty and fellows of the AFI Conservatory in Hollywood.

"The only reason so many people came to L.B. Mayer's funeral was to make sure he was dead."

- Anonymous

"The number one book of the ages was written by a committee, and it was called the Bible."

- Louis B. Mayer

(To a writer complaining of having to work with other writers.)

Top, L.B. Mayer with First Lady Eleanor Roosevelt, middle, with Helen Hayes, 1927 and bottom, being sworn in at the HUAC hearings in 1949.

Top, Mayer with Jean Harlow, middle, with George Bernard Shaw, Marion Davies and Clark Gable, bottom, MGM stars, John Howard, Cary Grant, Jimmy Stewart, and Katharine Hepburn teamed for 1940's The Philadelphia Story .

Top, Leo the Lion being recorded, middle, cast of 1939's The Women included Paulette Goddard and Norma Shearer and bottom, "Pops" gives away bride June Allyson at her wedding to Dick Powell.

Top, MGM's biggest box office stars of 1939, Mickey Rooney and Bette Davis, being crowned King and Queen of the Movies. Rooney loved such publicity, Davis hated it, middle, Esther Williams in Million Dollar Mermaid, bottom, Johnny Weismuller, Maureen O'Sullivan, Boy and Chita in a publicity still for the early Tarzan movies. At right, a 1946 group photo of MGM's biggest stars.

Top, Mervyn LeRoy (in white) with Richard Barthelmess, Jean Harlow, and Paul Muni, bottom, Arthur Freed (l.) with songwriting partner, Nacio Herb Brown.

3

First Things First

1. Samuel Goldwyn purchased the film rights for *The Wizard of Oz* from Frank Jayson Baum, "L. Frank Baum, Jr.," for $40,000 in 1934.

2. It was Goldwyn's intent to make a musical comedy film of *The Wizard of Oz* starring Eddie Cantor, however this plan never got past the idea stage.

3. Arthur Freed was a songwriter at MGM who had hopes of becoming a producer at the studio. Freed greatly admired the talents of the studio's teenage singer, Judy Garland. Freed himself asked Louis. B. Mayer for permission to develop a film specifically for Judy.

4. It was Arthur Freed who convinced MGM executives to purchase the film rights to *Oz* from Samuel Goldwyn, believing it a perfect vehicle to showcase Judy Garland.

5. MGM paid Samuel Goldwyn $75,000 for the final film rights to *The Wizard of Oz.* This agreement included the rights to all previous versions of the book.

6. Mervyn LeRoy, L.B. Mayer's newly-hired producer, (Mayer had successfully wooed LeRoy from rival Warner Brothers studio to replace Irving Thalberg who had passed away in 1936) was assigned to officially produce *The Wizard of Oz* along with Arthur Freed as assistant in February 1938.

7. At least sixteen writers worked on the *Oz* script including Irving Brecher, William H. Cannon, Herbert Fields, Samuel Hoffenstein, John Lee Mahin, Herman J. Mankiewicz, Jack Mintz, Ogden Nash, and Sid Silvers. Additionally, producer Arthur Freed, cast members Jack Haley and Bert Lahr and composer E.Y. Harburg contributed dialogue and ideas.

8. Noel Langley joined the *Oz* script team on March 11, 1938 and completed the first script on April 5, 1938. Langley received screen credit for his adaptation of *The Wizard of Oz*. Langley, with Edgar Allan Woolf and Florence Reyerson, received screen credit for their script.

9. An early outline of film characters included Dorothy, Aunt Em, Uncle Henry, Scarecrow, Tin Man, The Wizard, The Prince and Princess of Oz, and two witches. There was no mention of a lion.

10. John Mahin was an associate of Victor Fleming, well-versed in the art of rewriting scripts while a movie was being filmed. Mahin reworked the *Oz* script through early 1939 while the cast and crew filmed.

Over the Rainbow

• Arthur Freed had wanted Jerome Kern to do the music for *TWOO*, but Kern declined due to health reasons.

• Harold Arlen and E.Y. Harburg were signed to score *TWOO* in May 1938.

• The first *Oz*-related musical number written by the team of Arlen & Harburg was *The Jitterbug*, which was later cut from the film.

• *Over The Rainbow* was one of the last songs written for the film. Arlen recalled that the melody popped into his head one evening as he and his wife were driving home from the movies. Arlen made his wife stop the car in front of a drugstore where he sat and worked out the song.

• Upon hearing it for the first time, lyricist Harburg expressed displeasure with *Over The Rainbow*. (Alen had played the song for his partner in a flamboyant, majestic manner more suited to an operatic star than a teenage one.) It was only after Ira Gershwin suggested a less orchestrated arrangement for the song that Harburg was able to see its beauty.

Top, E.Y. Harburg and, right, Harold Arlen

Hats off to Noel!

Noel Langley joined the *Oz* script team on March 11, 1938 and completed the first script on April 5, 1938. Langley worked as both a writer and director on such projects as *Maytime*, *Edward, My Son*, *Scrooge*, *Ivanhoe, The Prisoner of Zenda, Tom Brown's School Days* and *The Pickwick Papers*. He also contributed, in an uncredited capacity, to *Listen, Darling*, Judy Garland's previous film to *Oz*. Langley passed away in 1980. It was Langley who would receive screen credit for the adaptation of *The Wizard of Oz,* and who created or further developed some of the most famous *Oz* elements including:

• Created the Kansas characters as real-life counterparts to the *Oz*-dream characters. Also created the idea of the entire *Oz* adventure being a dream.

• Created the idea for the stream of characters who fly by Dorothy's window as she sits in her bedroom riding inside the twister.

• Created the character of the comical Cowardly Lion and the horse-of-a-different-color.

• Further developed the talking/fighting apple trees, poisonous poppy field and its snow shower antidote from the original book.

• Had the Good Witch Glinda explain the magic in the ruby slippers, instructing Dorothy to "tap your heels three times...."

• Wrote the famous line, "Oh, Auntie Em, there's no place like home," as well as the dedication at the beginning of the film.

• It was Langley who changed the color of Dorothy's magical slippers from the original silver in the book, to ruby red. Langley did so simply because the red color would show up better on screen. This act of a color change accounted for the creation of the single most famous pair of footwear ever known.

...and a big thank you, also, to Woolf & Reyerson....

Although it was Langley's work that became the foundation for the *Oz* story on screen, two other writers, Edgar Allan Woolf and Florence Reyerson, were called in to rework Langley's script. The duo created the character of Professor Marvel, as well as his five-part *Oz* counterpart and added a few other discarded ideas and concepts. Although the Woolf-Reyerson script was also handed over to others for some additional reworking, it would be Langley, Woolf and Reyerson who would receive on-screen credit for the script.

4

"Dorothy"

1. *The Wizard of Oz* was purchased specifically as a vehicle for Judy Garland, who was a teenage contract singer/actress at MGM performing at studio functions, on radio and in small, but well-received, family films since 1935.

2. Although it was not officially announced until February 24, 1938, MGM had officially assigned Judy Garland to the role of "Dorothy" in late 1937. She was fifteen years old.

3. The press announced their selection of Judy as "Dorothy" while Garland was appearing live in an East Coast promotional tour for her film *Everybody Sing, released* in early 1938.

4. Judy was 15-years-old when it was announced that she would be Dorothy, and she was 16-years-old during the entire filming of the movie.

5. Judy received her regular salary of $500 per week for her work on *Oz*. In September 1935, Judy was signed to a standard MGM seven-year contract which started her at $100 per week. Regular increases had brought her to the weekly $500 mark by 1938.

6. It was during the filming of *The Wizard of Oz* that Judy was elevated from "featured player" to "star" status on the MGM roster in late November 1938. Judy was given her own portable dressing room which was brought to the *Oz* set, and a special ribbon cutting ceremony was held.

7. A story tells that director Victor Fleming nicknamed Judy, "Judalein," during the filming of *Oz*, however, birth and baptismal certificates indicate that this was a family nickname, (spelled Judaline), since May 1938 with the birth of Judy's niece who was named for her. Fleming and Garland would not meet until the last few days of October 1938.

Below, February 24th, 1938 newspaper announcement of Judy Garland's assignment as "Dorothy" in The Wizard of Oz.

THURSDAY, FEBRUARY 24, 1938

Judy Garland to Play Dorothy in Metro's 'Wizard of Oz' Film

SCRIPTS READY AND WAITING PAUL MUNI'S PERUSAL

Remember Dorothy, the Wizard, the Nome King and Belinda, The Amazing Hen from Frank Baum's Childhood Classics, the "Oz" books? Well, all these be-

the book for exhibition and he may let them have it for the motion picture exhibit.

* * *

Hot over the wire from New York comes a confidential mes-

8. After the success of *Oz*, L.B. Mayer tore up Judy's original 1935 contract, (which still had two plus years to go on it), and gave her a new contract increasing her salary to $2000 per week.

9. Judy suffered through a bad cold in early February 1939 that forced the production to virtually shut down for a week.

10. During rehearsals for the scene where Dorothy falls into the pig pen, Judy landed among some baby pigs whose full grown mother, also in the pen, immediately charged the young star. An assistant director quickly jumped into the pen and carried Judy to safety.

11. Three hours of school were required daily for Judy who was still taking high school lessons. As an adult, Judy would laughingly remember in exaggerated detail that, "They would call a break and I would rush to my teacher for five minutes of fractions, then go back to the set and do a scene, then back to the tutor for seventeen minutes of history. I ended up reciting more history in those scenes."

12. Judy went through ten "Dorothy" dresses in the course of filming of *The Wizard of Oz*.

13. Judy's stand-in/double during *The Wizard of Oz* was 29-year-old Bobbie Koshay, a seasoned film double and stuntwoman.

Surely, it was never Shirley!

The history of *The Wizard of Oz* is somewhat complex, but one fact remains: the part of "Dorothy" was always intended for Judy Garland.

Producer Arthur Freed sought to purchase the film rights to *The Wizard of Oz* expressly for Judy. Both Freed and Louis B. Mayer agreed to produce the movie as a vehicle to showcase young Judy's talents.

All of the MGM executives at the California studio believed Judy to be the perfect Dorothy. It was Loew's Theatres chief, Nicholas Schenck, in the New York City office, who did not believe that Judy possessed a "star name" big enough to carry off a film such as *The Wizard of Oz*, one that Schenck knew would cost the studio much money to produce and, therefore, would need a big name to ensure a good box office.

Because of this, Schenck directed MGM executives to at least approach Darryl F. Zanuck, head of the neighboring Twentieth Century Fox studios, about borrowing Shirley Temple, his studio's biggest star and the then most well-known child star.

It was arranged to have Roger Edens, Judy's music and vocal coach, visit Shirley at her studio in an attempt to casually test her vocal abilities. As cute and as popular as she was, Shirley could not really sing and it was obvious that she would not be able to carry off the musical numbers. MGM was able to easily convince Schenck that Shirley was unsuitable for the role.

Another story tells that *Oz* producers tried to arrange for a loan out of Jean Harlow and Clark Gable in exchange for Shirley, but this is impossible as Harlow had passed away in June 1937, months before MGM began formatting a production of *Oz,* and well before the arrival of *Oz* producer, Mervyn LeRoy, to the studio. (LeRoy started with MGM in early 1938.) Additionally, at no time was anyone other than Judy Garland ever announced by MGM or the press for the role.

"That entire production is precious to me. It all seemed like a fairy dream come true."

- Judy Garland commenting on The Wizard of Oz in 1950

14. In *The Wizard of Oz,* Dorothy is supposed to be a girl of about twelve. At age sixteen, Judy's blossoming figure was clearly evident. In order to give her body a less mature look, Judy wore a specially designed one-piece combination blouse/foundation that flattened her chest and reduced the appearance of her breasts. In the test photo above, it seems that Judy was not wearing the special undergarment as she is a far shapelier Dorothy than seen elsewhere in photos!

15. Contrary to what some have said, Judy's specially constructed foundation garment, while probably not all that comfortable, did not cause her any physical harm or injury. It also did not affect her singing voice as she was not wearing the garment when she recorded the songs for *Oz*.

16. During most of the filming of *The Wizard of Oz*, Judy wore the famous ruby slippers. The shoes were not the most comfortable of footwear and for rehearsals, Judy would often wear her ruby red *bedroom slippers* seen in the test shot at left.

Original still of deleted beehive scene involving the Tin Man

17. The character of Dorothy was initially envisioned as a glamorous, almost seductive, farm girl, complete with heavy makeup and long, blonde curls. Judy's makeup was eventually redone to a much lighter amount and, instead of a wig of blonde curls, her own reddish/brown hair was used.

18. Once Judy's own hair was utilized when her costume and makeup were changed, her own natural red highlights were emphasized with a special rinse, and a matching fall was attached to her shoulder length hair. Judy hated having to wear the fall because it took a half hour to attach each day.

19. Early in production, producers thought of changing the shape of Judy's nose by filling out its bridge with a small piece of rubber, but this idea was quickly discarded in favor of her natural nose.

20. Dorothy's blue and white gingham jumper had a light pink rinse added to it in order to improve the contrast of colors for the Technicolor process.

21. Dorothy's braids change length during the entire scene where she first meets the scarecrow.

The original version of Dorothy Gale was far different from the final film character.

A Tale of Two Dresses

A different colored "Dorothy" dress was made for Judy's stand-in to wear in the scene where Dorothy opens the door to Munchkinland. Stand-in Bobbie Koshay wore a black and white checked jumper with a light yellow rinse, while Judy wore the regular blue and white version. Koshay is seen with her back to the camera as she quickly walks to open the door. Koshay opens the door and steps backward and out of the shot, while Judy steps forward and into the shot. The use of the two actresses in one scene, coupled with their quick, seamless movement, created the illusion that it was one person. The different dress colors were necessitated by the limitations of the then brand new Technicolor process as the film shifted from black and white to color.

Judy and her stand-in, Bobbie Koshay, at the MGM commissary. Though almost identical in appearance, (stand-ins had to be the same height, weight and have the same coloring as a star), Koshay was actually thirteen years older than Judy.

22. Dorothy's new, more glamorous look after a visit to the Emerald City Brush-Up included false eyelashes, a touch of eyeshadow, and a soft rouge to her cheeks.

23. Because Judy was sixteen years old at the time that *The Wizard of Oz* was being filmed, the studio had to comply with certain rules regarding the use of minor children in films. One of these rules stipulated that all make-up and wardrobe had to be done at the child actor's home and not at the studio. Studio make-up and wardrobe people would arrive at Judy's home on McCadden Place in West Hollywood between 7:30 and 8:00 am each day and prepare the young star for her role. Judy would then be chauffeured to the studio, in complete costume and make-up, where she could begin filming between 9 and 9:30. This routine was followed for all of Judy's films until she reached eighteen years of age.

Hmmm....It seems Dorothy may have had a few choice words of her own for that apple tree that slapped her hand!

Several different "Dorothy" dresses were considered before settling on the simple blue & white check.

What they said about "Dorothy"....

Margaret Hamilton

"Oh, I just adored her!" remarked Margaret Hamilton about Judy Garland. "Judy was an absolute darling, a warm human being, and very professional. In the scenes between her and me, you see distress and fear in her eyes. Judy was just a young girl when she made the film. But there was a ladylike quality about her. Judy was one of the happiest people on the set, too. She was cooperative and fun. We chatted while we were in-between scenes. Judy was excited about her part in this picture. I think she realized it was going to be a wonderful thing in her career, as well. Everybody on the set loved her. She was busy, as she also had to attend school with a tutor during filming. She was just a darling and sweet person. She was a true sixteen-year-old. Not like some sixteen-year-olds who act as if they were sixty!"

Ray Bolger

"I had great admiration for Judy both as a person and a performer. Judy had a magic quality, a special presence. She liked to have fun, but once the cameras were rolling she was serious and dedicated. You'll read stories about how difficult Judy became to work with, but I never saw any evidence of that and I made two pictures with her. She was always so respectful of her fellow performers and the technicians. We never had any problems with her."

Jack Haley

"Judy was such a doll, a lovely person. She was as lighthearted a person as I ever met, and she was in seventh-heaven making the picture. You hear stories about her. But I never saw any of that. She was a lovely, happy young girl with impeccable manners. She was a wonderful person and it was a great pleasure working with her."

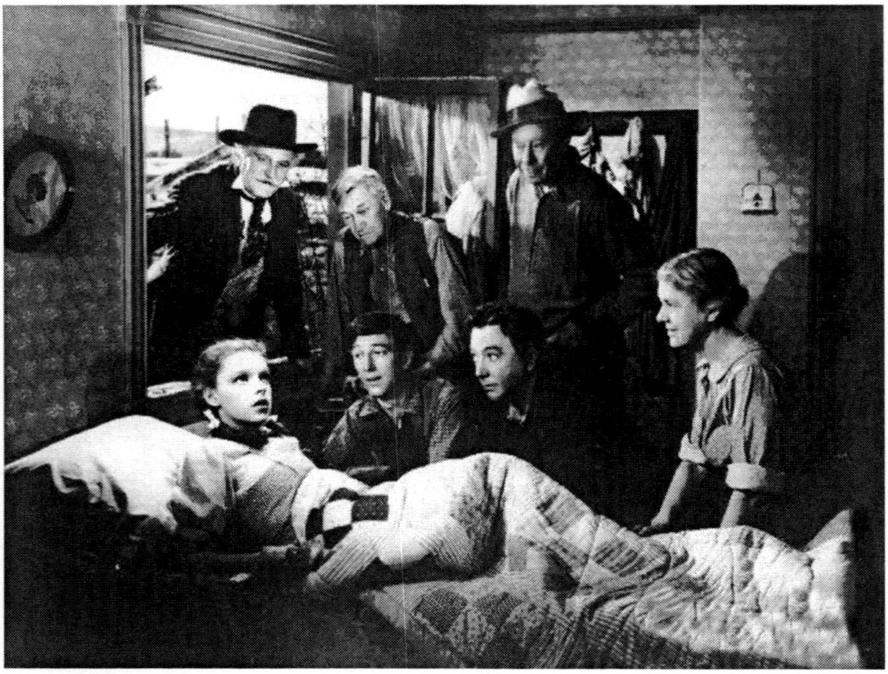

Above, "There's no place like home" and, below, the four friends.

5

...and her friends

"The Scarecrow"

1. Ray Bolger portrayed the Hunk/Scarecrow in the 1939 film version of *The Wizard of Oz*.

2. Bolger was originally assigned to play the Tin Man and Buddy Ebsen was cast as the Scarecrow. This greatly upset Bolger who maintained that when he signed his original MGM contract, he was promised the role of the Scarecrow in any film version of *Oz* that the studio might produce. After months of arguing with producers Freed and LeRoy, Bolger and Ebsen switched roles.

3. Ray Bolger was born January 10, 1904 in Massachusetts. A classic song and dance man, Bolger started in Vaudeville and later appeared on the Broadway stage. He signed with MGM in 1936.

4. In addition to *Oz*, Bolger co-starred with Judy Garland in *The Harvey Girls* from 1946.

5. Bolger had his own 1953 television sitcom and also appeared on numerous television shows, including *The Judy Garland Show* in 1963.

6. Bolger appeared live in several NYC nightclubs during the 1960's.

7. The Scarecrow's Kansas counterpart was named Hunk Andrews.

8. As the Scarecrow, Bolger had to wear a mask of baked rubber which gave his face the burlap effect.

9. Bolger's face mask wore out after just a few days wear. The actor went through forty masks during the course of filming *Oz*.

10. The Scarecrow's costume was fireproofed with asbestos, particularly important for the scene where the Wicked Witch sets fire to his arm in the castle.

11. Because of the Scarecrow's costume and the use of fire, a crew member always stood close by with a fire extinguisher.

12. MGM rented several large exotic birds for the Haunted Forest scene in *Oz*, one of which went after the straw in Bolger's costume - while the actor was in it! Bolger was forced to run from the set and into his dressing room until the offending bird could be caught.

13. The Scarecrow's Formula, the mathematical equation that the Scarecrow recites in order to prove his new brain, is supposed to be the famous Pythagorean Theory. It is in fact no theory since, as recited by the Scarecrow, it is mathematically incorrect.

14. The scene where the Scarecrow sings "If I Only Had a Brain" to Dorothy after they meet for the first time on the yellow brick road included an elaborate dance sequence performed by Bolger, much longer than what is seen. This extended dance performance was cut from the final film, something which Bolger said he did not know until he saw the film at its Hollywood premiere.

Left, Bolger demonstrates his style of "rubbery dancing" with his legs being able to do just about anything, this page, sharing the spotlight with a furry friend.

15. Bolger kept his Scarecrow costume and later donated it to The Smithsonian Institute.

16. Ray Bolger passed away on January 15, 1987 at age 83.

"We may not receive any residuals from The Wizard of Oz, but the film gave us something far greater; it gave us a sort of immortality."

- Ray Bolger

"The Tin Man"

1. Buddy Ebsen was announced to play "The Tin Woodsman" in *The Wizard of Oz* on January 31, 1938. Ebsen had appeared in several MGM films, including in *Broadway Melody of 1938* in which he danced with Judy Garland.

2. Like the Scarecrow, Cowardly Lion, and Wicked Witch, Ebsen's original costume as the Tin Man called for no facial make-up. This was soon changed when it was decided that the *Oz* characters had to be all fantasy.

3. Ebsen's make-up called for a white-face clown effect, over which was applied, in powder form, an aluminum dust which gave him the "tinny" look.

Jack Haley with Shirley Temple and Alice Faye at 20th Century Fox

5. After six weeks of inhaling the aluminum dust used for his make-up, Ebsen's lungs became coated with the material, effectively suffocating him. Ebsen recalled, "One evening at home, I felt myself incapable of drawing a breath and had to be rushed by ambulance to the hospital." Ebsen remained under doctor's care for several weeks.

6. Jack Haley was secured for the part of the Tin Man on a loan-out from 20th Century Fox Studios.

7. Jack Haley was born August 10, 1898 in Boston, Massachusetts. Haley appeared in Vaudeville, on stage, and on radio. In films, he usually played second leads who were silly, but very likeable. He appeared with Judy Garland in *Pigskin Parade*.

8. The Tin Man's Kansas counterpart is named Hickory Twicker.

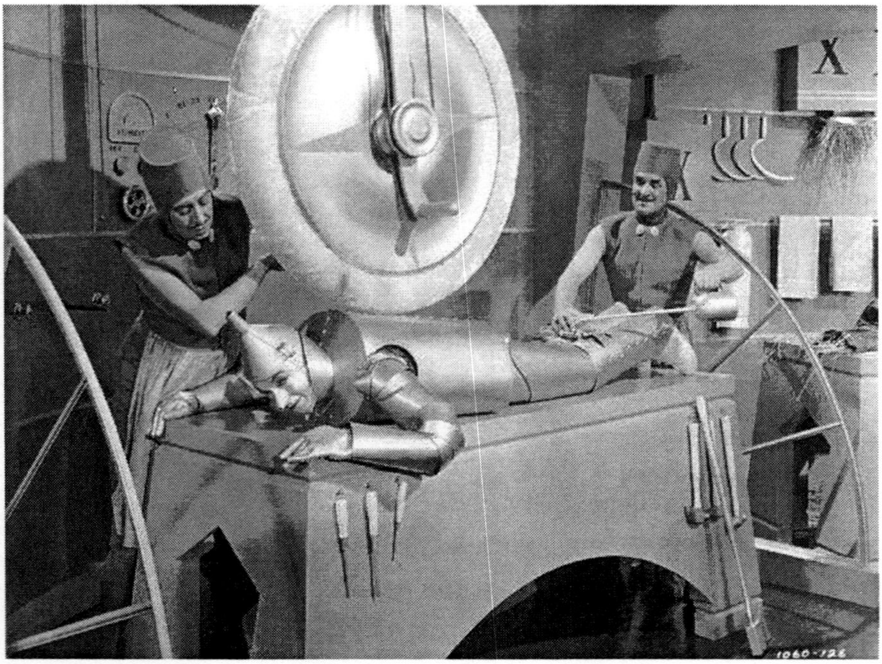

9. In an early version of the *Oz* story, The Tin Man was cast as a sort of womanizer with an eye for Glinda, The Good Witch of the North.

10. Because of the problems with the powdered aluminum make-up, MGM developed a cream paste that would achieve the same "tinny" look when Haley took over the role.

11. After a few weeks in the role, Haley developed a serious eye infection from the cream paste and was forced to spend several days in a darkened room while the infection healed.

12. Haley's "tin" costume weighed about forty pounds and prevented him from sitting down. Because of this, a specially padded slant board was constructed for him against which he could rest.

13. In the first filming of the scene involving the Tin Man, Haley's costume was a bright, shiny silver. It was later realized that this was not in keeping with the Tin Man's line, "I've been standing over there rusting for the longest time." Haley's costume was immediately "rusted" and the sequence redone. The Tin Man would not get his shine back until the "Brush-up" scene in Emerald City.

14. The "oil" used on the Tin Man was actually chocolate syrup.

15. Haley's last appearance was with Ray Bolger at the 1979 Academy Awards where the duo presented an award. Haley passed away on June 6, 1979.

"The Cowardly Lion"

1. Bert Lahr was signed to play The Cowardly Lion in September 1938, but had actually begun work on the film that August.

2. Bert Lahr was born Irving Lahrheim on August 13, 1895 in New York City. Lahr appeared in Vaudeville and on the New York stage. Said Lahr, "If you want to be a success in Hollywood, be sure and go to New York."

3. Lahr made his stage debut (bottom) in 1917 as part of *The Best Show in Town* on the burlesque circuit.

4. Once it was determined that the role of the Cowardly Lion would be played by a man in a lion costume, (and not, as once thought, by an actual lion with a dubbed voice), it was *Oz* lyricist E.Y. Harburg who recommended Bert Lahr for the role. He had worked previously with Lahr, and knew his comedic style would suit the role perfectly.

5. The Lion's costume consisted of about fifty pounds of actual lion skins plus padding which brought the costume's weight up to about seventy pounds.

6. Lahr's costume was unbearably hot, (the actor was also clad in a full suit of "long-johns") causing the actor to perspire terribly inside the suit. Tiny holes were inserted throughout the suit, but did little to reduce the heat factor. As a result, Lahr would unzip the costume any time that the cameras stopped rolling. From time to time, Lahr would have to completely remove the costume in order to allow it - and himself - to dry out from the perspiration.

One of the all time greatest deliveries of a line in a motion picture; Bert Lahr as the Cowardly Lion: "Put 'em up, put'em up."

7. Lahr, Haley and Bolger arrived at the studio for makeup just before seven each morning. Lahr refused to sit for more than an hour's makeup each day.

8. The Cowardly Lion's Kansas counterpart was named "Zeke."

9. The Cowardly Lion's tail could not "stand up" or "wag" on its own and, when necessary for a particular scene, a worker would walk along a catwalk constructed above the set, following Lahr through a scene and manipulating the lion's tail, which was attached to a pole with fishing line.

10. Lahr as The Cowardly Lion, ad-libbed many lines, mostly culled from his Burlesque days, but which were ultimately deleted. His most famous was, "Peculiar weather we're having, ain't it?" during the poppy field scene.

11. Bert Lahr died on December 4, 1967 in New York City from pneumonia. Judy Garland was appearing in concert at the time and was so shocked at Lahr's death that she cancelled that evening's performance. At her next performance, she dedicated *Over the Rainbow* "to my dear Cowardly Lion."

"After I made Oz, I was typecast as a lion, and, you know, there aren't all that many parts for lions."

- Bert Lahr

Above, Lahr with co-star Charlotte Greenwood in 1931's Flying High. Bottom, Lahr received the 1964 Tony award for Best Actor in a Musical for his role in "Foxy." Left to Right are, Sir Alec Guinness, Sandy Dennis,Carol Channing, and Lahr.

"Glinda, The Good Witch"

1. The original *Oz* outline called for "two witches," one of which was "The Good Witch," seen as a sort of comical witch. Two of the era's popular female comedi-ennes, Fanny Brice and Beatrice Lillie, were considered for the role, but it would be Billie Burke who would take the part.

2. Billie Burke was born Mary William Ethelbert Appleton Burke on August 7, 1883, in Washington, D.C., the daughter of Billy Burke, a professional and internationally renowned clown. Burke and her family toured the world with the circus before settling in England where she first appeared, to rave reviews, on the London stage.

Burke with husband Florenz Ziegfeld & daughter Patricia.

3. Burke was 55-years-old when she filmed her part in *Oz*.

4. Burke played many roles in both films and on stage, but was best known for her portrayal of the "dizzy, dipsy, upper-class matron." Burke was also well-known for her role in the *Topper* series of comedies from the 1930's and '40's.

5. Glinda, the Good Witch of the North was actually a composite of the two good witches in L. Frank Baum's original story. In Baum's book, the Good Witch of the North was a little old lady. The other good witch was Glinda, the beautiful, young witch who lived in the red-colored Quadling County near Oz.

6. Judy Garland and Billie Burke portrayed mother and daughter in the 1938 film, *Everybody Sing*.

7. Billie Burke appears in *Oz* for a total of twelve minutes.

8. Burke used a photo of herself as Glinda, The Good Witch of the North as her Christmas card for decades after *Oz*.

"Age doesn't matter, unless you are a cheese."

- Billie Burke

9. Burke wore a wig of long blonde curls over her own shorter red hair.

10. Burke was the second wife and widow of the famous showman, Florenz Ziegfeld, who died in 1932. Myrna Loy (bottom) portrayed Burke in the MGM film, *The Great Ziegfeld.*

11. Although Burke's time on the *Oz* set was limited, she insisted on having all the trappings of the star she was brought to the set including a well-appointed trailer/dressing room and many assistants.

12. During work on *Oz*, Burke sprained her ankle. The star insisted on an ambulance and press coverage of the minor injury.

13. Burke was 77 years old when she made her final screen appearance as Cordelia Fosgate in *Sergeant Rutledge* in 1960. Burke later suffered from Alzheimer's Disease and passed away from natural causes on May 14, 1970 in Los Angeles.

"The Wicked Witch of the West"

1. The "second witch of Oz" was first described as an ugly old woman, then conceived of as an evil, but stunningly beautiful, female.

2. Three names were mentioned in connection with the Wicked Witch: Edna Mae Oliver, Margaret Hamilton and Gale Sondergaard.

3. Margaret Hamilton tested for the part early on, (as the first ugly witch), but learned she did not get the part when she read that Sondergaard had been cast, and that the witch had been changed in style from ugly and bad, to beautiful and bad.

4. Sondergaard, a dark-haired beauty who had already won an Oscar for Best Supporting Actress, was cast in the role of the Wicked Witch of the West and outfitted in a slinky, black, form-fitting, sequined head-to-toe body suit.

Gale Sondergaard in the original costume for the Wicked Witch.

5. As the role of the Wicked Witch was restyled back to an old, ugly crone, both Sondergaard and MGM realized that the actress' overwhelming natural beauty would preclude her from playing the part convincingly, and Sondergaard happily left the cast of *Oz*.

6. Margaret Hamilton had previously played the Wicked Witch of the West of the 1903 stage version, in local community theatre.

7. Hamilton was born on December 9, 1902 in Cleveland, Ohio. She held an undergraduate degree and license as a kindergarten teacher.

8. Was divorced from Paul Meserve and had one son, Hamilton.

9. Because false nails had not yet been developed, the fingernails of the Wicked Witch of the West were cut from pieces of clear film negative, painted green, then

glued to Hamilton's fingers. If the actress moved too quickly, the fake nails would suddenly pop off.

10. Margaret Hamilton suffered severe burns on her face and hands when, during the scene in Munchkinland when the witch disappears in a cloud of orange smoke, the flame effect shot up and ignited the actress' costume, as well as activated the oils in her green makeup to a boil. Hamilton's makeup had to be excruciatingly removed with alcohol against her already burned skin.

11. Hamilton was forced out of production for six weeks while she received medical treatment for her severe burns. When asked, many years later, why she didn't sue MGM, she replied, "Oh, I could never do that. Not if I wanted to ever work as an actress in Hollywood again."

12. Margaret Hamilton continued to perform until her death in May 1982 from a heart attack. In her later years she appeared as "Cora" in commercials for Maxwell House Coffee.

13. Hamilton's cackle as the Witch was so shrill that it broke tubes on the recording devices.

One of the scariest shadows ever cast

"Auntie Em & Uncle Henry"

1. The first actress considered for the role of "Auntie Em" was May Robson, who declined the part because she believed it undemanding and unimportant.

2. Actress Sarah Padden was also tested, but the part went to fifty-seven-year-old Clara Blandick.

3. Clara Blandick was born June 4, 1881 on an American ship in Hong Kong where her parents worked. Blandick spoke Chinese before she spoke English.

4. Blandick was primarily a stage actress and entered films at age 33.

May Robson, the first considered for the role of Auntie Em, with child actors, Edith Fellowes, Mickey Rooney, Freddie Bartholomew and Judy Garland in 1936.

5. Auntie Em/Clara Blandick is the only *Oz* cast member not listed in the opening credits of *The Wizard of Oz*.

6. At the age of eighty, and suffering severe illness, including blindness, Blandick committed suicide by taking an overdose of pills and pulling a plastic bag over her head. It is said that Blandick came home from church on Easter Sunday 1962, put on her best clothes, arranged all her favorite possessions around her, then took her life.

7. Charley Grapewin was the first choice for the role of Uncle Henry. At the time of *Oz* casting, Grapewin was set to retire from films, and Harlan Briggs was named for the role. Grapewin had a change of heart about retiring and was assigned to play Uncle Henry. Grapewin finally retired in 1952.

9. Grapewin was born December 20 in 1869 and died on February 2, 1956.

10. Grapewin was married forforty-seven years to Anna Chance. They had no children.

11. Entered films at the age of 60, playing old characters in rural settings. Also known for his role as "Grandpa Joad" in 1940's *The Grapes of Wrath*.

12. Grapewin played with Judy Garland in 1938's *Listen, Darling*.

"The Wizard"

1. Although Frank Morgan was Arthur Freed's first choice to play the Wizard, producer Mervyn LeRoy favored Ed Wynn. Wynn was offered the role, (when it did not yet feature the four alter-egos of the Wizard), but turned it down because he felt it was too small and brief.

2. Others considered for the role of the Wizard included, Wallace Beery, (he put himself up for the role), W.C. Fields, (a serious consideration, but salary could not be agreed upon) Hugh Herbert, Victor Moore, Robert Benchley and Charles Winninger.

3. Frank Morgan was born, Francis Philip Wuppermann, on June 1, 1890 in New York City and died on September 18, 1949.

4. Member of the Phi Kappa Psi Fraternity, comprised of "honorable men, courteous and cultured....seeking intellectual, moral and spiritual excellence."

5. Judy Garland appeared previously with Morgan on radio and later would be teamed with him in *Annie Get Your Gun*, a film which Garland did not complete and during which Morgan passed away.

"If Disney can reproduce people with cartoons, then we can reproduce cartoons with people."

- Oz producer Mervyn LeRoy

Two Wizards? Wallace Beery (right) playing cards with Frank Morgan in the film 'Madelon. Beery put himself up for the role of the Wizard that Morgan was awarded. Below, Frank Morgan in the MGM anti-Nazi melodrama, The Mortal Storm, (starring Jimmy Stewart and Margaret Sullavan) the story of a German family torn apart by World War II. The movie caused the Nazis to ban the showing of all MGM pictures in Germany and its occupied territories.

6

...and Toto, too!

1. Toto was a female Cairn terrier whose real name was Terry. Terry was a pure breed born in 1933. Terry's named was "officially" changed to Toto after the success of *The Wizard of Oz.*

2. Toto's trainer was Carl Spitz, a world-renowned animal handler.

3. Spitz opened the Hollywood Dog Training School in 1927. It was located on Riverside Drive in North Hollywood.

4. Until Toto, Spitz's most famous dog was Buck, the St. Bernard from *Call of the Wild,* starring Clark Gable.

5. Spitz obtained Toto from a couple who found the dog too high strung and hard to handle.

6. Toto's first movie role was with Shirley Temple and Jane Withers in the 1934 film, *Bright Eyes*.

7. Toto also appeared in *Ready for Love*, *Bad Little Angel*, *Fury* (with Spencer Tracy), *The Buccaneer* and *Barefoot Boy*.

8. Mervyn LeRoy originally intended for the role of Toto to be played by an actor in a dog costume. There was some debate also over whether or not to give Toto the ability to talk in the film.

9. In the 1902 stage version of *The Wizard of Oz*, Dorothy's companion was not a dog, but a cow named Imogene. The cow was portrayed by a man in a cow costume.

10. Toto has nine close-ups and barks forty-four times in *The Wizard of Oz*.

11. Toto suffered a sprained paw after being stepped-upon by one of the Winkie Guards while filming the scene in the witch's castle. Because of the sprain, a stand-in dog was very briefly used.

12. A stuffed toy Toto was used for one or two sequences. (See page 82.)

13. After *The Wizard of Oz*, Toto's next film appearance was in the first scene of the 1939 release, *The Women*, followed by several other movies for different studios.

Above, Toto, still known then as Terry, with child actresses Shirley Temple and Jane Withers in the 1934 film, Bright Eyes.

14. Toto died in 1945 and was buried in the backyard of The Carl Spitz Hollywood Dog Training School. The land was later upturned for development of the Ventura Highway.

Top, Oz director Victor Fleming with Jean Harlow and, bottom, with producers Freed and LeRoy and other Oz designers.

7

Production #1060

1. MGM assigned *The Wizard of Oz* the production number of 1060. This number appears on all reference material and photos.

2. It took almost eight months to format the MGM production of *Oz*, including casting, sets, wardrobe, script, etc. Actual filming on *Oz* began on October 12, 1938.

3. *The Wizard of Oz* was filmed entirely on soundstages 24, 25, 26 and 27 at the MGM Culver City studios. Soundstage 26 was used primarily for filming.

4. *Oz* had a total of four official directors in the course of its production: Richard Thorpe, George Cukor, Victor Fleming and King Vidor.

5. Victor Fleming is the director of credit for *The Wizard of Oz.*

6. According to some records, just prior to the appointment of Thorpe as director of *Oz*, Norman Taurog was announced as the film's director, working with *Oz* for three days before being reassigned to *Huckleberry Finn*. Others maintain, however, that Taurog was simply helping out with *Oz* before starting *Huck Finn,* to which he had already been assigned.

7. Richard Thorpe was a well-respected director whose 183 film credits include numerous westerns and adventure films including the *Tarzan* series of pictures.

8. Thorpe spent one month working on *Oz*. It was Thorpe who created the "baby doll" image of Dorothy Gale, complete with heavy makeup and a wig of long blonde curls, and directed Judy Garland to act in an affected manner.

9. After seeing Thorpe's initial work, producers LeRoy and Freed were horrified and immediately fired Thorpe. It was announced that Thorpe had "taken ill" and would not be returning to the *Oz* set.

10. George Cukor was called in to give a new direction to *Oz*. Everyone

knew that Cukor's stay with *Oz* would be very short since he was waiting to begin directing his own film, *Gone With the Wind.*

11. Cukor was with *Oz* for only one week, but he is credited with putting into place several important and well-known elements of *Oz*. It was Cukor who redeveloped Dorothy's look and manner, getting rid of all of Judy's heavy makeup and curls as well as the affected attitude. Cukor emphasized Judy's natural appearance and told her not to act in a "fancy-shmancy way" and to "just be yourself."

12. Victor Fleming arrived to the *Oz* set on October 30 and remained with the production until February 17, 1939 when he left to take over the reigns of *Gone With the Wind.*

13. King Vidor, a director, writer, producer and actor, whose career stretched from 1916 until 1991, was hired to direct the Kansas farm scenes including the famous *Over the Rainbow* music sequence.

14. Bobby Connolly was the dance director for *Oz*, brought in over Busby Berkeley.

Previous page, Richard Thorpe on the set of Apache and, left, George Cukor, c.1935

15. Because *Oz* was such a unique film, many of the studio's employees wanted to visit the set. A guard was posted at the stage doors and only contract players were permitted entry to visit the *Oz* set.

16. The Wicked Witch, the Lion, the Tin Man and the Scarecrow were asked not to eat lunch in the MGM commissary as their fantastic costumes and makeup distracted too many MGM employees who complained that they could not enjoy their meal.

17. The vast majority of the scenery in *Oz* was actually painted canvas, including most of the yellowbrick road, the poisonous poppy field, Kansas farm and Emerald City.

18. The Kansas scenes in *Oz* were not meant to be viewed in black and white. The Gale farm was indeed filmed in black and white, but the film negatives of these scenes were then colored in sepia in order to give them a dry, brownish tint.

19. Jack Dawn was in charge of the make-up for *Oz*. An army of both seasoned make-up professionals and newly-hired apprentices were assigned to the demanding task of meticulously applying the *Oz* designs day after day.

King Vidor and script girl Betty Hill on the set of The Wedding Night in 1935.

20. Each of the Winkie Guards had to be at least six feet in height and were made up to look exactly alike. There labored, guttural voices were achieved by recording adult voices at normal speed, then playing them back at a slower speed. Conversely, no two Munchkins could look alike and their high-pitched voices were made by recording normal adult voices, then playing them back at high speed.

21. Billie Burke, as Glinda, wore "cosmetic lifts," an early form of a face lift. These lifts were fine silk glued near the ear, then pulled and secured tightly in order to correct sagging flesh.

22. Glinda comes and goes via a large pink bubble. There was, of course, no real bubble, only a silver Christmas ball and some trick photography.

23. Three hundred extras were used to inhabit Emerald City.

A view of the Oz set while filming the Munchkinland scene

Munchkin Magic

• There were officially 124 Munchkins. Hired under the name of The Singer Midgets, the Munchkins were little people corralled from all parts of the country and overseas to work for Leo Singer, a well-known producer of "midget shows" in Vaudeville. Singer had won the contract to supply the little people for MGM.

• Stage personnel were assigned to aid the little people with such tasks as maneuvering onto and off the elevated sets and platforms and on furniture, as well as assisting them in the standard-sized bathrooms.

• The male Munchkins all wore bald caps with individually designed hair-pieces, dyed various colors of the rainbow. No two Munchkins could have the same facial makeup, unless they were part of a group.

• Some Munchkins were designated for specific spots including The Mayor, The Barrister, The Town Crier, The Coroner, 3 Lullaby League Girls, 3 Lollipop Guild Boys, 1 General, 6 soldiers and 5 fiddlers.

• For Christmas 1938, Judy Garland arrived to the set of *Oz* with several pounds of chocolate candies for the Munchkins, as well as autographed pictures of herself for them.

• Over the years stories of Munchkin mayhem have become popular, highlighting the little people's supposed penchant for alcohol and ungentlemanly conduct. These stories, however, have been greatly distorted and there were few real instances of problematic or unseemly behavior among the group.

"Judy was a beautiful and kind young woman, and an all-American teenager. She was nothing but nice to us."

· Jerry Maren, who portrayed the Munchkin member of 'The Lollipop Guild' who hands Dorothy the lollipop.

24. The view of Emerald City was actually a painted-on canvas backdrop. Tiny holes were made through the green towers in order to let the light shine through and provide the twinkling effect.

25. The poisonous poppy field was created with a painted backdrop along with 40,000 red and pink paper poppies inserted into a set piece. It took twenty men one week to insert all the paper flowers.

26. The snow shower that broke the Wicked Witch's sleep spell was created by sprinkling the set with gypsum dust. The actors were advised not to inhale too deeply as the material was irritating and potentially toxic.

27. The Gale home seen inside the twister was actually only 3 feet high. The floor of the house was painted to look like the sky, the house was then filmed dropping to the sky-painted floor. The film was then run in reverse in order to obtain the effect of the twister taking the house skyward.

Far left, one of Dorothy's dresses going to auction in 1970. This page, the Tin Man balloon at the 1939 Macy's Thanksgiving Day Parade.

28. The twister was actually a muslin sock, combined with many other elements including wire, wind machines, smoke, several cameras and a crane.

29. All of the costumes for the citizens of Emerald City had, of course, to be emerald green. The MGM wardrobe department assigned several workers to do nothing but dye clothing and other material just the right shade of green.

30. The *Oz* costumes were designed by Gilbert Adrian, credited always as "Adiran," who was married to MGM actress Janet Gaynor.

31. The Winged Monkeys were actually costumed actors. There were about two dozen actors costumed as the Winged Monkeys. The "army' of monkeys flying by the window of the witch's castle were actually miniature toy models.

32. Several of the monkey-costumed actors suffered injuries when the wires from which they were suspended broke "in flight."

33. The Winged Monkeys actually carried off Judy Garland's stunt double.

34. The scene where the witch flies off from her castle window used a doll pulled on a track.

35. The *Oz* set was lighted by more than 350 huge electric lamps. The heat from the lamps was often unbearable and after a scene was completed, the crew would open the soundstage's huge doors and the wind machines would be turned on in order to circulate much needed air.

36. The *Oz* production needed far more electricity than what the California power company could provide in the existing MGM facility, so a separate power station was built close to the set in order to generate what was needed.

37. The house that falls on the Wicked Witch of the East was actually a small, one-sided facade and not actually an entire house.

38. The legs of the Wicked Witch of the East were inflated bicycle tire inner tubes, painted with white stripes and wearing a pair of ruby slippers. The disappearance of the legs in the Munchkinland scene was achieved simply by deflating the tubes which made the "legs" curl up.

39. On screen, the Wicked Witch of the West disappears from Munchkinland in a cloud of orange smoke, but was actually lowered on an elevator-type platform.

40. The talking apple trees were made of lightweight wood and rubber with zippers down their bark backs which allowed for actors to climb inside.

41. *The Wizard of Oz* finished filming on March 16, 1939, but post-production work including sound effects, dubbing, retakes, etc, lasted until June 1939.

42. *The Wizard of Oz* cost a total of 2,777, 000 making it MGM's most expensive film made to that date.

43. MGM spent $250,000 on the *Oz* promotional tour including a nearly four week live appearance tour by Judy Garland at the Capitol Theatre in NYC.

44. *The Wizard of Oz* premiered on August 15, 1939 at Grauman's Chinese Theatre and on August 17, 1939 at the Capitol Theatre in New York City.

45. *The Wizard of Oz* was copyrighted on August 7, 1939.

46. The initial sneak preview of *Oz* was in June 1939 at San Bernadino, Ca.

Judy Garland and Mickey Rooney arrive at NYC's Grand Central Station on August 14, 1939 for the NYC premiere at the Capitol Theatre.

47. It was after the second sneak preview at Pomona that *Over the Rainbow* was removed from the film. MGM executives believed it was demeaning to have one of their stars sing in such a drab setting as a barnyard and they also believed the sequence slowed the picture down.

48. Producers Feed and LeRoy threatened to walk from MGM if *Over the Rainbow* was not reinserted into the film. The song remained in the film and went on to win the Academy Award for Best Song.

49. Although *Oz* received rave reviews, especially for Judy Garland, the film's initial theatrical release brought in only $3, 017,000. This was due mainly to the fact that the vast majority of the film's patrons were children who paid an average of just ten cents to see the film.

50. The radio debut of *The Wizard of Oz* was on June 29, 1939 on The Maxwell House Hour radio show hosted by Robert Young.

51. *The Wizard of Oz* appeared on television for the first time on November 3, 1956 on the CBS network. It was hosted by Bert Lahr and 10-year-old Liza Minnelli. Liza's mom watched the show from her dressing room at the Palace Theatre in NYC where she was in the middle of an extended run.

52. The first television showing of *TheWizard of Oz* in 1956 drew a 53% share of the nationwide viewing audience.

53. The second television showing of *The Wizard of Oz* was in December 1959 and was hosted by Red Skelton and his daughter.

54. Annual television showings began with the 1959 airing. Subsequent hosts included Dick Van Dyke, Richard Boone and Danny Kaye. Hosts for the show were discontinued after 1967, except for a special tribute made to Judy Garland by Gregory Peck before the 1970 showing, the first after Judy's death.

Original advertisement for the New York City release of Oz.

The Ruby Slippers

• The ruby slippers were originally silver in color, but were changed due to the fact that red would show up better on screen, especially against the yellow brick road.

• The ruby slippers were simple "school girl pumps," covered in material, rhinestones and sequins. They cost less than $10.

• There were probably ten pairs of ruby slippers made, but only five are actually known to be in existence today.

• The ruby slippers were used as part of a publicity campaign for the movie in 1939. A pair of the slippers was awarded as the grand prize in a contest for school kids. The shoes were won by ten-year-old Roberta

Bauman who held onto the shoes until 1988 when they were auctioned off for $165,000. These shoes were re-auctioned in 2000 for more than $600,000.

• A pair of ruby slippers are on permanent loan/display at The Smithsonian Institute in Washington, D.C.

• An early shoe was created in an elfin-like style (below) known as the Arabian test shoes. Actress Debbie Reynolds owns this pair and had them on display at one time in her Hollywood Museum.

• Two other pairs are definitively known to be owned by private collectors. Two additional pairs of ruby slippers are *said* to be in the hands of private collectors, but these have never been seen.

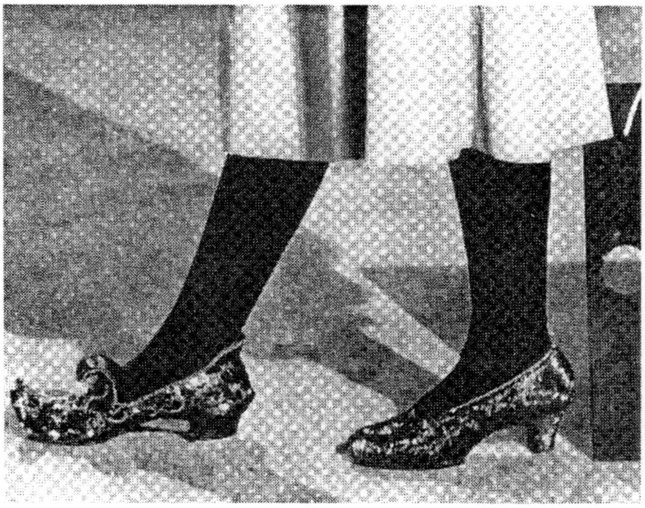

The Capitol Theatre on Broadway and 51st Street in New York City on August 17th, 1939, the opening day of The Wizard of Oz.

8

The Film

The following odds and ends may be found as you watch The Wizard of Oz. Included are descriptions of numerous ***filmed but deleted scenes****, which, if they had remained in the film, would have added even more charm to an otherwise already wonderful film, as well as established several key reference points in the film.*

1. The dedication at the beginning of the film used to be cut from television in order to allow the film to run in the allotted time period.

2. In the early television presentations, the Kansas scenes used to be in black and white, not sepia.

3. **Filmed but deleted scene**: After Auntie Em hushes Dorothy while counting the chicks, she and Uncle Henry discuss Dorothy's situation referring to her as, "Poor little orphan..."

4. Filmed but deleted scene: After Hunk hits his finger with the hammer, the next scene was supposed to be inside the barn where Hickory is showing Dorothy his new invention, a machine that breaks up winds. When he turns on the motor, oil spurts all over his face. In the same scene, Hickory complains that he has lots of aches and pains, as if his joints were all rusted. He goes on to tell Dorothy that Miss Gulch is just a "poor old maid who hasn't any heart left. He advises Dorothy to "have more heart" and take pity on Miss Gulch. Dorothy replies that "I try to have a heart."

5. After Dorothy falls into the pig sty, she comes out all clean. This, of course, was due to the magic of the movies, however, such magic was not in place during rehearsals as evidenced by a story told by Judy's mother, Ethel Gumm, concerning Judy' work at the studio: "The other day she arrived home from rehearsals covered with dirt. It was in her hair, on her face. She looked terrible. She said, 'I had to lie down in a pen with pigs all day and let them root at me!'"

6. The bridge over which Dorothy walks as she approaches Professor Marvel's wagon is the same bridge over which Scarlett O'Hara drives her wagon in *Gone With the Wind*.

7. Filmed but deleted scene: As Dorothy and Professor Marvel talk, she asks him to take her and

Toto with him, saying that no one cares about her at home, that they wouldn't even miss her and that Auntie Em even let Miss Gulch take Toto from her.

8. **Filmed but deleted scene:** After looking at the picture he has taken from Dorothy's basket, Professor Marvel comments on the poppies on the wallpaper in Dorothy's bedroom, setting up the scene for the poisonous poppy field.

9. **Filmed but deleted scenes:** As the storm picks up force, Dorothy can't decide what to do. She says that if they go back to the farm, the sheriff will take Toto away, but Auntie Em could be dying and she has to get to her. She decides to go back to the farm and hide Toto.

10. The original script called for Miss Gulch to throw the basket containing Toto into the river where it is shown floating along in the water, then Toto escapes from the basket and safely swims to shore, then makes his way back to Dorothy.

11. **Filmed but deleted scene:** As the storm starts, Hickory runs to the barn where he has his wind machine, but Uncle Henry stops him and tells him to go help Hunk with the horses.

Original lobby cards from the 1939 release.

12. In the scene where Dorothy walks out of the house after it lands in Munchkinland, *in the sequence where the viewer only sees her from behind as she walks through Munchkinland*, she is carrying a "stuffed" Toto. (As you watch the dog from behind, it makes no movement, is small and oddly shaped.)

13. Making the pond in Munchkinland blue proved a challenge. The first attempt to achieve this effect was to add blue coloring, but this turned everything in the water blue. The inside of the pond was then painted blue which gave it the appearance of blue water.

14. Judy had to fake watching Glinda's pink bubble descend into Munchkinland since, of course, there was no real bubble. Notice that Toto has no reaction to the bubble since he does not see anything.

15. The house that fell on the Wicked Witch of the East was actually a one-sided facade.

16. The bricks in the yellowbrick road were originally oval and the road did not have a curb.

17. A munchkin ascends to the yellowbrick road via a manhole which is never seen again at anytime on the yellowbrick road.

18. The munchkin mayor adjusts the padding for his stomach several times throughout the Munchkinland scene.

19. After the Wicked Witch of the West appears in Munchkinland, she has several filmed but deleted lines that are particularly vicious, including telling Dorothy, "I'm here for vengeance."

20. If you look closely as the witch prepares to leave Munchkinland, you can see the little trap door open and close through the smoke.

21. Filmed but deleted: The scene where the Scarecrow sings "If I Only Had a Brain" to Dorothy after they meet for the first time on the yellowbrick road, included an elaborate dance sequence performed by Bolger, much longer than what is seen. This extended dance performance was cut from the final film, something which Bolger says he did not know until he saw the film at its Hollywood premiere.

22. Just after Glinda kisses Dorothy good-bye, she lightly hits herself in the head with her wand as she motions towards the Munchkins. You can hear the sound of the wand tinkle against the crown.

Giggles & giggles & giggles...Oh, my!

Over the years, a story has been passed along concerning Victor Fleming and his choice of technique for eliciting the correct response from young Judy while filming the above scene where Dorothy slaps the lion's nose, reducing the King of The Forest to tears. According to the accounting, an exasperated Fleming, frustrated by Judy's repeated giggling at the lion's crying, slapped the young star in the face in order to get her to maintain her composure. This story was recounted by only one person and never even mentioned by anyone else associated with *Oz*, including Judy Garland and the other actors and crew.

Munchkin player Jerry Maren clearly remembered the scene saying that Judy would indeed repeatedly break up over the Lion's crying, but that she was able to camouflage it herself by pulling Toto close to her face during the scene. In the actual film, you can clearly see Judy stifling her laughter by pressing Toto close to her face. Additionally, not only is it highly unlikely that a director of Fleming's stature would have resorted to slapping a young girl, (such type of direction has never been mentioned in connection with Victor Fleming on any film), but it is equally unlikely that Judy would have responded in any positive manner to this type of treatment or that her mother or MGM executives would have just let such an incident pass.

23. Real corn stalks were originally used in the Scarecrow's cornfield until the heat from the huge lamps withered the stalks almost immediately. Fake stalks were then substituted for the real stalks.

24. In the scene involving the talking trees, just after the tree starts to throw apples, watch Dorothy closely as she jumps backwards and you can see that she is not wearing the ruby slippers, but rather a pair of black flats or slippers.

25. The apples on the talking apple trees were made of rubber.

26. Throughout the entire Tin Man sequence, Dorothy holds one apple, two apples, one apple, no apples, one apple, etc, all in the same scene.

27. When the Tin Man toots his funnel cap during his dance, Toto becomes frightened and runs away.

28. Filmed but deleted scene: After the Scarecrow and Dorothy invite the Tin Man to join them on their journey to Emerald City, the Tin man hesitates at first, saying that it is a long and dangerous journey and it might rain along the way. The Scarecrow reminds him

Advertisements for The Wizard of Oz appeared for weeks before the actual release of the film.

how much he wants a heart and Dorothy assures him that she will keep the oil can in her basket. This is just before the Tin Man's line, "Well, suppose the Wizard wouldn't get me one when we got there?"

29. Filmed but deleted scene: After the Tin Man puts out the fire with his funnel, the Witch sarcastically wishes Dorothy good luck with the Wizard and on her trip back to Kansas.

30. Filmed but deleted scene: Just after the Tin Man says, "Just try and let her make a beehive out of me," bees start appearing from the Tin Man's body. He swats a bee dead, then starts to cry that he has, "...killed that poor little honey bee. Only a man without a heart could do that." Dorothy comforts him by telling him that it wasn't a honey bee, but "an old drone bee that was about to die." Dorothy assures the Tin Man that he did a good thing because he put the bee out of his misery.

31. Filmed but deleted scene: Immediately after the beehive scene, Dorothy then suggests that the two characters should leave her alone because the witch might harm them. The two men refuse to leave her side. Dorothy then goes into her "You're the two best friends anybody ever had" speech.

32. "Lions and tigers and bears" was originally a longer, repetitive sequence.

33. The lion that jumps from the rock onto a hidden trampoline and then onto the yellowbrick road was actually Bert Lahr's stunt double.

34. **Note**: Dorothy never once tells the Scarecrow, Tin Man or Lion her name.

35. **Filmed but deleted scene:** After Dorothy and the Lion lie down in the poppy field, the scene switches to the Wicked Witch who says to the Winged Monkey, "Bring me my wishing cap. I'll call the Winged Monkeys to fetch me those slippers." This cap is in reference to the wishing cap in L. Frank Baum's original book which had a secret jewel inside the brim that you held while reciting a special incantation that allowed the owner to call upon the Winged Monkeys. In the next scene, which remains in the film, the Witch is holding a gold cap with red stones which she ultimately throws across the room. Once the previous scene in which she asks for the wishing cap was deleted, the cap became just a meaningless prop with no reference point in the film.

36. Although you never hear it in the film, the commander of the Winged Monkeys is named "Nikko" (see film credits). Also deleted from the film is the explanation as to why Nikko's

Mickey Rooney and Judy Garland arrive at Grand Central Station in New York City in August 1939 for the live promotional event at the Capitol Theatre.

wings are smaller than the those of other monkeys. When the Wicked Witch captured Nikko, she clipped his wings in order to make him more subservient to her (he is unable to fly away from her). Nikko's wings are indeed clipped in the film, but we never learn why.

37. As the foursome and Toto skip out of the poppy field, (serenaded by the song *Optimistic Voices*), Dorothy loses her footing, but manages not to fall by hanging onto the Lion.

38. Two white horses were alternately used for the horse-of-a-different-color scene. The horse did not achieve his colorful status from actual dye, but rather was sponged down with either gelatin in different flavors or vegetable dye.

39. Filmed but deleted scene: The horse-of-a-different color was also seen in light blue and pink.

40. The carriage that is used to transport the group through Emerald City was actually used by Abraham Lincoln himself during his presidency.

41. Filmed but deleted scene: Just after the Wicked Witch skywrites her message, Dorothy points to the sky and says, "It's the Wicked Witch, she's followed us here." In an amusing but deleted line, the Tin Man responds, "Can't that female take no for an answer?"

42. Filmed but deleted scene: The witch's famous skywritten message was actually filmed as "Surrender Dorothy or Die, WWW."

43. The scene where the lion jumps out of the window in the throne room of the Wizard was again done by a stuntman.

44. Filmed but deleted scene: As the group enters The Haunted Forest, the Lion is holding a large net and an oversized spray gun

Judy and Mickey dance at the Waldorf-Astoria party held in their honor

Judy and Mickey needed a police escort through Grand Central Station

labeled "Witch Remover." He hands the spray gun to Dorothy saying she can use his witch remover to keep the witch away. Scarecrow takes the spray gun from Lion and throws it on the ground. The spray gun disappears as it hits the ground, then the net flies out of Lion's hands. This prompts Scarecrow's line, "I believe there's spooks around here"

45. Filmed but deleted scene: In the scene where the Wicked Witch orders the Winged Monkeys to go after the group, she says, "They won't give you any trouble; I've sent a little insect on ahead to take the fight out of them." This is in reference to the "jitterbugs" that swoop down on the foursome while they are in the haunted forest, nipping at them and causing them to break out into the deleted "Jitterbug" song and dance routine. Portions of this scene in rehearsal were filmed as home movies and are available on certain editions of the DVD and videotapes of the film.

Death on the yellow brick road?

This one just keeps hangin' around!

In recent years, a favorite rumor that keeps recirculating is that a male munchkin or stagehand suffering through a bout of unrequited love, hanged himself on the set during the filming of *The Wizard of Oz,* and his death was captured on-camera and used in the final print.

This "suicide" scene occurs as Dorothy, the Scarecrow, and the Tin Man head down the road in the forest on their way to the Emerald City. In order to give the indoor set of the forest a more realistic look, several birds of various sizes were rented from a local zoo and allowed to roam the set. At the very end of this sequence, as the three main characters move down the road and away from the camera, one of the larger birds moves around and spreads its wings. No hanging, just a big bird flapping its wings.

What is most amusing about this story, often recounted with numerous embellishments, is that it is simply impossible to believe that a human being could have hanged himself on a movie set and yet none of the hundreds of people present, including actors, directors, cameramen, technicians, and many more, would or could have failed to notice or react to the occurrence.

Additionally, in order for such an act to have made it into the final print of a movie, it would also have had to have been overlooked by all the directors, editors, film cutters, technicians, and others who worked on the film in post-production. And even if by some (very) wild chain of events an incident such as this did indeed happen as described, does anyone think it would have been left intact in one of the most famous films ever made and seen over and over again for more than sixty-five years?

46. **Filmed but deleted scene:** The scene where Scarecrow is found torn apart on the ground by Tin Man and Lion was originally longer with the three characters exchanging several humorous lines as they try to reconstruct the Scarecrow. (Tin Man: "I wish I were better at doing puzzles.")

47. **Filmed but deleted scene:** In the witch's castle, when Dorothy is alone, she sings a short reprise of *Over the Rainbow*, her voice laden with sobs. One reason why this scene was cut was because it was believed that it would be too traumatic for children.

48. **Filmed but deleted scene:** Several times during the chase inside the castle, the Wicked Witch of the West hits her Winkie Guards with her broom which explains why the Winkies were so glad to give Dorothy the witch's broom. Deleted lines included the Winkies cheering that she can't hit them anymore with her broom.

49. The scene where the Wicked Witch melts away was done with another trap door special effect. The Witch's costume was nailed to the floor, air and dry ice were blown upwards and she was lowered down into the floor on a small elevator platform while her dress and hat remained above.

50. **Filmed but deleted scene:** After Dorothy liquidates the Wicked Witch, all of Emerald City joins the group in an elaborate parade known as The Triumphant Procession. The four characters joyfully march back into Emerald City, the Scare-crow holding the witch's broom high overhead, accompanied by a rousing chorus of *Ding, Dong, The Witch is Dead.*

51. Filmed but deleted scene: The scene where Dorothy taps her heels three times and repeats, "There's no place like home," was accompanied by a recap of scenes from Dorothy's dream played in reverse order and ending with the landing of the house back in Kansas and the close-up of Dorothy in her bed, which was kept intact.

An original 1939 ad for Oz and the original Decca soundtrack.

Then again, maybe not...

The following were ideas that were discarded, some faster than others, from the proposed Oz screen adaptation and/or script.

• An opera-singing Prince and Princess of Oz.

• A budding romance between Hunk and Dorothy.

• A talking horse-of-a-different-color.

• The Scarecrow, Tin Man and Lion using the horse-of-a-different color as transportation to the witch's castle where Dorothy is locked up.

• Auntie Em going after Miss Gulch to get Toto back.

• A niece and/or son for a Mrs. Gulch.

• A son for the Wicked Witch.

• A female worker on the farm who is a love interest for Hickory in Kansas and later the Wizard's assistant in *Oz*.

• A dwarf or giant companion for Professor Marvel.

• A rainbow bridge in *Oz* that is another a trap set by the Wicked Witch.

• A slapstick scene where the foursome have to construct a human pyramid to enter the Wizard's throne room through a window.

• A battle of bravery between the Cowardly Lion and a dragon, a gorilla or another lion.

Test your Ozzie.I.Q.

All of the answers to the following quizzes may be found in either this book or in the actual film. Quizzes are of varying difficulty.

= Easy

= Easy & Hard

= Harder

Could you have worked at MGM in 1939?

1. In what year was the MGM studio formed?

2. Who were the three partners?

3. Where was the studio located?

4. Who was the MGM mascot?

5. What is the MGM motto?

6. What theatre chain owned MGM?

7. Where were its (the theatre chain) headquarters?

8. Who was its (the theatre chain) president?

9. What did Mama Mayer contribute to MGM?

10. How many soundstages did MGM have?

11. Which name associated with MGM first purchased the film rights to the *Oz* books from L. Frank Baum?

12. Who were the two MGM producers assigned to *TWOO*?

13. How much did MGM pay for the final film rights to *TWOO*

14. Who bought MGM in 1970?

15. Who purchased the MGM film library in 1986?

16. Who owns the MGM classic film library now?

Answers: 1.1924, 2. Samuel Goldwyn, Louis B. Mayer and Marcus Loew, 3. Culver City, CA, 4. Leo the Lion, 5. "Ars Gratia Artis", 6.Loew's, 7. NYC, 8.Nicholas Schenck, 9.recipes, 10. 28, 11.Goldwyn, 12. Arthur Freed & Mervyn LeRoy, 13. $75,000, 14. Kirk Kerkorian, 15. Ted Turner, 16. Warner Brothers

According to Louis B. Mayer, MGM had more of these than in the heavens....

...Stars!

Yep, they were all under contract to MGM. Can you match the star with the movie in which he or she starred? Some were hits, some were flops.HINT:You can obtain assistance at www.imdb.com.

1. Judy Garland	A. *The Public Enemy*
2. Mickey Rooney	B. *Flying Down to Rio*
3. William Powell	C. *It Happened in Brooklyn*
4. Myrna Loy	D. *The Big Hangover*
5. Johnny Weismuller	E. *Roberta*
6. Jimmy Stewart	F. *Thoroughbreds Don't Cry*
7. Frank Sinatra	G. *Madame Curie*
8. Fred Astaire	H. *Knute Rockne*
9. Ginger Rogers	I. *Rosalie*
10. Gene Kelly	J. *Captains Courageous*
11. Elizabeth Taylor	K. *The Three Muskateers*
12. Lucille Ball	L. *Libeled Lady*

13. Jean Harlow	M. *The Mortal Storm*
14. Esther Williams	N. *Dancing Lady*
15. Clark Gable	O. *Easy to Wed*
16. Greta Garbo	P. *White Cargo*
17. Bette Davis	Q. *Glory*
18. Jimmy Durante	R. *Picture of Dorian Gray*
19. Robert Taylor	S. *That Hagen Girl*
20. Mario Lanza	T. *Meet Me in St. Louis*
21. Lassie	U. *Mata Hari*
22. Margaret O'Brien	V. *The Human Fish*
23. Angela Lansbury	W. *Bachelor & Bobby-Soxer*
24. Walter Pidgeon	X. *Boom Town*
25. Greer Garson	Y. *Johnny Eager*
26. Claudette Colbert	Z. *Look Who's Laughing*
27. Shirley Temple	AA. *The Little Foxes*
28. Ronald Reagan	BB. *Lassie Come Home*
29. Eleanor Powell	CC. *The Student Prince*
30. Lucille Bremer	DD. *The Kissing Bandit*

1-F, 2-J, 3-L, 4-W, 5-V, 6-M, 7-DD, 8-B, 9-E, 10-K, 11-D, 12-Z, 13-A, 14-O, 15-N, 16-U, 17-AA, 18-C, 19-Y, 20-CC, 21-BB, 22-Q, 23-R, 24-P, 25-G, 26-X, 27-S, 28-H, 29-I, 30-T

For the kiddies

These are easy-to-answer trivia questions for younger fans.

1. What is the name of the little girl in *The Wizard of Oz*? *Dorothy*

2. In what state does she live? *Kansas*

3. With whom does she live? *Auntie Em & Uncle Henry*

4. What is the name of her dog & what color is he? *Toto, black*

5. What does Dorothy fall into on the farm? *a pig pen*

6. What does Dorothy sing about on the farm? *a rainbow*

7. What color is Dorothy's dress? *blue and white check*

8. Who comes to take Toto? *Miss Gulch*

9. In what does she put Toto? *a basket*

10. When Dorothy runs away, whom does she meet? *Professor Marvel*

11. Why does Dorothy return to the farm? *Auntie Em might be sick*

12. What whisks Dorothy & Toto away? *a twister*

13. Where does Dorothy land? *Munchkinland*

14. On whom does Dorothy's house land? *Wicked Witch of the East*

15. What does everyone tell Dorothy to follow? *the yeloowbrick road*

16. Who is the first character that Dorothy meets on the yellowbrick road? *Scarecrow*

17. Of what is the Scarecrow afraid? *fire*

18. What do Dorothy and the Scarecrow pick? *apples*

19. Who is the second character that Dorothy meets? *Tin Man*

20. What doesn't the Tin Man have? *a heart*

21. What two things does the Tin Man always have with him? *oil can & ax*

22. What does the Wicked Witch throw at the Scarecrow? *a ball of fire*

23. What do Dorothy, the Scarecrow & the Tin Man chant as they walk through the Haunted Forest? *Lions & Tigers & Bears*

24. Who do they meet in the forest? *The Cowardly Lion*

25. What does the Scarecrow want from the Wizard? *a brain*

26. What does the Tin Man want from the Wizard? *a heart*

27. What does the Lion want from the Wizard? *courage*

28. What does the group have to cross? *a poppy field*

29. What kind of a spell is over the field? *sleep*

30. What breaks the spell? *it snows*

31. Where does the Wizard live? *Emerald City*

32. What animal changes color? *a horse*

33. What does the group have to get to earn their gifts from the Wizard. *the broomstick of the Wicked Witch of the West*

34. Who attacks the group in the forest? *the Flying Monkeys*

35. To where do they take Dorothy? *witch's castle*

36. Whom does Dorothy see in the witch's crystal ball? *Auntie Em*

37. Who chases the group through the castle? *The Winkie Guards*

38. How does Dorothy kill the Wicked Witch? *she throws a bucket of water on her*

39. The Wizard is really what? *an ordinary man*

40. What does the Wizard give the Scarecrow? *a diploma*

41. What does the Wizard give the Tin Man? *a heartshaped watch*

42. What does the Wizard give the Lion? *a medal*

43. How do Dorothy and the the Wizard try to get home? *in a balloon*

44. Who comes to Dorothy's aid after the Wizard leaves? *Glinda*

45. What does Dorothy have to do to get home? *click her heels together*

46. Where is Dorothy when she wakes up? *in her bedroom*

47. What does Dorothy say at the end of the movie? *"There's no place like home."*

Who said it? #1

1. "Oh, Toto, there's no place like home." *Dorothy*

2. "Perfect? Bang on my chest if you think I'm perfect." *Tin Man*

3. "Pay no attention to that man behind the curtain!" *The Wizard*

4. "I'll get you, my pretty...and your little dog, too!" *Wicked Witch*

5. "Some people without brains do an awful lot of talking." *Scarecrow*

6. "We must be over the rainbow!" *Dorothy*

7. "That dog is a menace to the community." *Miss Gulch*

8. "Are you a good witch or a bad witch?" *Glinda*

9. "Find a place where you won't get into any trouble." *Auntie Em*

10. "I haven't got any courage at all!" *Lion*

11. "Follow the yellow brick road." *The munchkins*

12. "I do believe in spooks. I do, I do, I do believe in spooks." *Lion*

13. "Well, bust my buttons!" *Oz Doorman*

14. "Now, that's a horse-of-a-different-color." *Oz Cabbie*

15. "Who rang that bell?" *Oz Doorman*

16. "...tap your heels together three times." *Glinda*

17. "All in good time, my pretty, all in good time." *Wicked Witch*

18. "But if you please, what are munchkins? *Dorothy*

19. "We can't go against the law, Dorothy." *Auntie Em*

20. "Toto, I have a feelimg we're not in Kansas anymore." *Dorothy*

In Kansas with Auntie Em & Uncle Henry

1. She takes care of Dorothy. Auntie Em

2. Toto is put inside this. basket

3. Miss Gulch's mode of transportation. bicycle

4. What Toto did to Miss Gulch. bite

5. What Auntie Em & Uncle Henry are counting. chicks

6. This large animal flies by Dorothy's window. cow

7. Another word Dorothy uses for a twister. cyclone

8. The Tin Man's Kansas name. Hickory

9. The Scarecrow's Kansas name. Hunk

10. What went bad on the Gale farm. incubator

11. She doesn't like Toto. *Miss Gulch*

12. What Dorothy falls into. *pig sty*

13. He has a crystal ball. *professor marvel*

14. The Lion's Kansas name. *Zeke*

15. Miss Gulch hit Toto with this. *rake*

16. Two men in this go by Dorothy's window. *rowboat*

17. Miss Gulch has an order from him to take Toto. *sheriff*

18. Dorothy says that Auntie Em can send her to bed w/o this. *supper*

19. Professor Marvel's horse is named this. *Sylvester*

20. He's Dorothy's dog. *Toto*

21. This blew threw the farm. *Twister or cyclone*

22. He takes care of Dorothy & Auntie Em. *Uncle Henry*

23. Hunk, Zeke & Hickory are fixing this on the farm. *wagon*

24. This blows in on Dorothy during the storm. *window*

Complete the lyric

1. "Ding, dong, the wicked witch is dead. She's gone

where the goblins go, below, below, below....

2. "I could while away the hours, conferring with the flowers

consulting with the rain....

3. "Someday I'll wish upon a star

And wake up where the clouds are far behind me.

4. "Where troubles

melt like lemon drops

5. "We get up at twelve and

start to work at one...

6. "I'm afraid there's no denyin'

I'm just a dan-de-lion.

7. "Ding dong, the witch is dead

Which old wict?, The wicked witch

8. "When she fell out of Kansas,

a miracle occured

9. "You're off to see the wizard

the wonderful wizard of Oz

10. "I'd be tender, I'd be gentle,

and awful sentimental

11. "Each rabbit would show respect to me

the chipmunks genuflect to me

12. "Birds fly over the rainbow

why then, oh why can't I

13. "With the thoughts you'd be thinkin'

you could be another Lincoln

14. "I'd be friends with the sparrows

and the boy who shoots the arrows

15. "Yes, it's sad believe me, Missy

when you're born to be a sissy

16. "We can make a dimple smile out of a frown

Can you even dye my eyes

to match my gown?

17. "That's how we laugh the day away

In the merry old land of Oz

18. "I could stay young and chipper

and I'd lock it with a zipper

19. "Just then the witch, to satisfy an itch

went flying on her broomstick,

thumbing for a hitch

20. "The house began to pitch, the kitchen took a slitch, it landed on the Wicked Witch

in the middle of a ditch

Who said it? #2

1. “I’m a little muddled.” *Glinda*

2. “You call that long?” *Wicked Witch*

3. “I’ve got a plan.” *Scarecrow*

4. “What a smell of sulfur.” *Glinda*

5. “She was hungry!” *Talking Apple Tree*

6. “Of course we won’t.” *Uncle Henry*

7. “It’s a good thing it wasn’t your head.” *Zeke*

8. “Do you know any?” *Professor Marvel*

9. “Everybody into the storm cellar.” *Uncle Henry*

10. "Oil can what? *Scarecrow*

11. "Arf! Arf! Arf! *Toto*

12. "I can cause accidents, too!" *Wicked Witch*

13. "Hail to Dorothy!" *Winkies*

14. "Jiminy Crickets" *Dorothy*

15. "I wanna go home!" *Lion*

16. "Silence,whippersnapper!" *Wizard*

17. "These things must be done delicately." *Wicked Witch*

18. "It's always best to start at the beginning." *Glinda*

19. "You humbug!" *Scarecrow*

20. "I'll bring a damage suit that'll take your whole farm." *Miss Gulch*

21. "Well, that's just you all over" *Tin Man*

Match up the cast and crew

1.Thorpe	A. He handled Toto.
2. LeRoy	B. He adapted the screenplay.
3. Ebsen	C. The director of briefest stay.
4. Fleming	D. He wrote the music to *Oz*.
5. Blandick	E. On loan out from Fox Studios
6. Dawn	F. He was the last to direct *Oz*.
7. Cukor	G. The original Tin Man.
8. Lahr	H. She wanted out of her role.
9. Walshe	I. Billie was married to him.
10. Gilbert	J. He was a NYC stage actor.
11. Bolger	K. He's better known as Adrian.

12. Ziegfeld	L. The director who was let go.
13. Haley	M. He started it all.
14. Vidor	N. Head of Winged Monkeys
15. Sondergaard	O. He is the director of credit.
16. Baum	P. He was the producer of *Oz*.
17. Langley	Q. Spoke fluent Chinese.
18. Spitz	R. The second Tin Man
19. Arlen	S. He did the *Oz* makeup.

1-L, 2-P, 3-R, 4-O, 5-Q, 6-S, 7-C, 8-J, 9-N, 10-K, 11-G, 12-I, 13-E, 14-F, 15-H, 1 6-M, 17-B, 18-A, 19-D

Oz by the numbers

Each of these answers is in mumber form or relates to a number. Answers may be found both in the film and in this book.

1. In what year was *The Wizard of Oz* released? *1939*

2. When Auntie Em is counting the chicks, what number is she up to when Dorothy arrives home? *58*

3. How many directors did *Oz* have? *4*

4. What was the total number of Munchkins represented by *The Singer Midgets*? *124*

5. For how many years has the Tin Man been rusting? *1*

6. How much did MGM pay for the film rights to *Oz*? *75,000*

7. How old was Judy Garland during the filming of *Oz*? *16*

8. How many extras were used to inhabit Emerald City? *300*

9. How many soundstages did MGM have in 1939? *28*

10. How many times does Dorothy have to tap her heels together? *3*

11. How many times does Toto bark in the film? *44*

12. What number soundstage was *Oz* primarily filmed on? *26*

13. What was the production # assigned to *Oz*? *1060*

15. In what year did the NYC stage version of *Oz* premiere? *1903*

16. How many theatres did Loews own in the NYC area? *26*

17. How many Dorothy dresses were made for Judy Garland? *10*

18. What is the numerical date for the copyright of *Oz*? *08/07/1939*

19. How much did the ruby slippers cost to make? *$10*

20. How many parts does Frank Morgan play in the film? *5*

21. What was Judy Garland's weekly salary for *Oz*? *$500*

22. How many minutes does Billie Burke appear in the film? *12*

24. What was the total production cost of *Oz*? *2,777,000*

25. How many hours does Dorothy have to live in the witch's castle *1*

Improve your Ozzie Vocabulary

We give your a rather obscure Oz word & the person who said it, you supply the rest of the line. (We also give you the meaning.)

1. "jabber-wapping" - Auntie Em

What's all this jabber-wappin?
Mmeaning: nonsense talk

2. "buffalo" - Zeke

You going to let that old Gulch heifer buffalo
you? Meaning: intimidate

3. "Duroc" - Zeke

Dorothy fell in with the big Duro
Meaning: a huge hog that bites

4. "pusillanimous" - Wizard

Why, every pusillanimous creature
Meaning: weak

5. "aver" - Munchkin Coroner

As coroner, I must aver
Meaning:affirm, attest to

6. "bide" - Wicked Witch

Very well, I'll bide my time, Meaning: wait

7. "sulphur" - Glinda

Pooh-What a smell of sulphur.
Meaning: an odor like smoke

8. “mettle” - Tin Man

When a man's an empty kettle, he should be on his mettle.
Meaning: strength

9. “sissy” - Lion

When you're born to be a sissy
Meaning: coward

10. “prowess” - Lion

But I could show my prowess
Meaning: abilities

11. “horse of a different color” - Oz cabbie

Now, that's a horse of a different color
Meaning: A different matter

12. “savoir-faire” - Lion

That certain air of savoir-faire
Meaning: class

13. “caliginous” - Wizard

You clinking, clanking collection of caliginous junk
Meaning: dirty, rusty

14. “effrontery” - Wizard

You have the effrontery to ask for a brain.
Meaning: rudeness

15. “bovine fodder” - Wizard

You billowing bale of bovine fodder
Meaning: food for a cow

Test your Ozzie I.Q.

Here are 100 questions designed to test your knowledge of the 1939 film version of "The Wizard of Oz." ***The questions run in the order of the film****, so you easily check your answers just by following the film. The questions are of varying difficulty, so all ages can answer. Need help, contact us at* ***oztriviabook@aol.com.***

1. Who is the only cast member not mentioned in the opening credits?

   Clara Blandick

2. What are the very first words spoken as the film begins?

   She isn't coming yet, Toto

3. What is the name of the little girl in *TWOO* and what is the name of her dog?

   Dorothy

4. Who is bothering Dorothy and her dog?

   Miss Gulch

5. Who are Dorothy's guardians?

   Aunte Em & Uncle Henry

6. What is Dorothy's last name?

   Gale

7. Who played the role of Dorothy?

   Judy Garland

8. What was Toto's real-life name?

   Terry

9. In early television presentations of *TWOO*, what part of the film was cut out?

   The opening dedication

with 100 Questions

10. What are Auntie Em and Uncle Henry doing when Dorothy arrives home? *counting chicks*

11. According to Dorothy, how often does Toto get into Miss Gulch's garden? *"just once or twice a week"*

12. What has gone bad on the farm? *the old incubator*

13. What are the names of the three farm hands? *Hunk Andrews, Hickory Twicker, Zeke*

14. What are the farmhands fixing on the farm? *a wagon*

15. Which farmhand does not have a last name? *Zeke*

16. What does Zeke call Miss Gulch when he says, " You gonna let that old Gulch.....buffalo you?" *heifer*

17. What does Auntie Em offer the farm hands to eat? *crullers*

18. What does Dorothy fall into and who saves her? *pig sty, Zeke*

19. What does Miss Gulch have strapped to the basket of her bicycle? *an umbrella*

20. What did Toto do that got Miss Gulch upset? *he chased her cat and, got into her garden and bit her leg*

21. What does the mailbox on the gate say? *Gale*

22. What is Uncle Henry doing when Miss Gulch arrives? *painting the fence*

23. What is Miss Gulch's first name? *Almira*

24. What is Auntie Em doing when Miss Gulch arrives? *knitting*

25. What does Miss Gulch hand Auntie Em? *the sheriff's order*

26. What alternative to destroying Toto does Auntie Em offer Miss Gulch? *keeping him tied up*

27. For how many years has Auntie Em been wanting to tell Miss Gulch what she thinks of her? *23*

28. How much of the county does Miss Gulch own? *half*

29. According to the outside of his wagon, by whom is Professor Marvel acclaimed? *crowned heads of Europe*

30. What hangs above the interior doorway of Professor Marvel's wagon? *skull*

31. What food is Professor Marvel cooking ? *a hot dog*

32. What kind of dress is Auntie Em wearing in the photo that Professor Marvel takes from Dorothy's basket? *polka dot*

33. What illness did Dorothy have during which Auntie Em stayed by her side every minute. *measles*

34. What is the name of Professor Marvel's horse? *Sylvester*

35. What kind of a storm does Professor Marvel say it is? *a whopper*

36. Who says, "It's a twister! It's a twister! *Zeke*

37. Who is the first one inside the storm cellar? *Auntie Em*

38. Who is the last one inside the storm cellar and the one who closes the door? *Hunk*

39. What flies off of the house in the storm? *screen door*

40. What farm animals fly past Dorothy's window? *cow and chickens*

41. Where does Dorothy's house land? *Munchkinland*

42. What color are the stockings that the Wicked Witch of the East is wearing when the house lands on her? *black & white striped*

43. Who is the first person to greet Dorothy? *Glinda*

44. How does Glinda travel? *in a pink bubble*

45. What is the first thing that Glinda asks Dorothy? *Are you a good witch or a bada witch?*

46. According to the Munchkin Mayor's watch, what time is it when Dorothy arrives in Munchkinland? *five o'clock*

47. What is the name of the league that greets Dorothy? *Lullaby*

48. What is the name of the guild that greets Dorothy? *Lollipop*

49. How does Dorothy bid good-bye to the Munchkin Ballet? *She blows a kiss*

50. According to the Munchkin Coroner, what kind of dead is the Wicked Witch of the East? *most sincerely dead*

51. According to the song, *Ding Dong, The Witch is Dead*, where does the wicked witch go? *where the goblins go*

52. According to the Munchkins, "This is a day of independence, for all the Munchkins...." and who else? *their descendants…if any*

53. What color smoke signals the arrival and departure of the Wicked Witch of the West? *orange*

54. Glinda warns the Wicked Witch to "Begone..." before what happens to her? *someone drops a house on you, too*

55. How many individual Munchkins tell Dorothy to "Follow the yellowbrick road?" *four*

56. According to the Scarecrow's song, what President would he be like if he had a brain? *Lincoln*

57. What does the talking tree do to Dorothy when she picks an apple from his branch? *slaps her hand*

58. When did the Tin Man get caught in the rain chopping the tree? *"about a year ago"*

59. According to the Tin Man's song, what two emotions does he want to feel? *jealousy and devotion*

60. In the forest, what does Dorothy have in her basket? *oil can, apples, coverlet*

61. How many times does the trio repeat "Lions and tigers and bears?" *four*

62. What does the Cowardly Lion call the Tin Man? *a shivering junkyard*

63. What does the Cowardly Lion call the Scarecrow? *a lopsided bag of hay*

64. What does the Cowardly Lion call Toto? *pee-wee*

65. What is the Cowardly Lion afraid to count? *sheep*

66. What does the group have to walk across in order to reach Emerald City? *the poisonous poppy field*

67. What kind of a spell does the Wicked Witch of the West cast on the group as they cross the poisonous poppy field? *sleep spell*

68. How is the spell broken and by whom? *Glinda sends a snow shower*

69. What color is the horse-of-a-different-color when we first see it in Emerald City? *white*

70. What three other colors does the horse become? *orange, yellow, purple*

71. How does Dorothy introduce herself to the Wizard?
I am Dorothy the small and meek

72. What do Dorothy and her friends have to do to gain their wishes from the Wizard? *get the broomstick of the WWW*

73. What message does the Wicked Witch write in the sky? *Surrender Dorothy*

74. What was the name of the Wicked Witch's guards? *The Winkies*

75. What was the name of the Wicked Witch's army? *The Winged Monkeys*

76. On the sign in The Haunted Forest, what word is spelled incorrectly ?
"witches," it should be witch's

77. Who leads the trio of characters to Dorothy after the Winged Monkeys take her away? *Toto*

78. Who first sees the Winkie Guards come up behind them? *The Lion*

79. How does the trio outwit the Winkie Guards?
They pretend to be guards and join the line.

80. What does the Wicked Witch throw at Dorothy and her friends?
her hourglass

81. What does the Scarecrow do to stop the Winkie Guards from attacking them? *He cuts the rope holding the chandelier*

82. What do the Winkie Guards chant when they realize that the Wicked Witch is dead? *Hail to Dorothy! The Wicked Witch is dead!*

83. Who reveals the Wizard as just a man behind a curtain? *Toto*

84. What does the Scarecrow call the Wizard? *You humbug!*

85. What degree does the Wizard give the Scarecrow? *ThD: Doctor of Thinkology*

86. What does the Wizard make the Lion a member of? *The Legion of Courage*

87. What time is it on the heart-shaped watch that the Wizard gives the Tin Man? *12:10*

88. What color is the Wizard's bag? *black*

89. For whom did the Wizard work before he landed in Oz? *The Miracle Wonderland Carnival Co.*

90. To what land does the Wizard say he and Dorothy will return? *E Pluribus Unum (USA)*

91. What city is named on the Wizard's balloon? *Omaha*

92. Why does Toto jump out of Dorothy's arms? *He sees a cat.*

93. According to Glinda, how long will it take the ruby slippers to get Dorothy home? *two seconds*

94. How does the Tin Man know that he now has a heart? *because he says it's breaking at having to say goodbye*

95. Whom does Dorothy tell that she will miss him most of all? *The Scarecrow*

96. How many times does Dorothy have to tap her heels together in order to go back to Kansas?

three

97. What is Auntie Em doing to Dorothy in order to wake her ?

putting a cold cloth on her head

98. Back in Kansas, who is the first person from *Oz* that comes to check on Dorothy?

The Wizard/Professor Marvel

99. What does Uncle Henry say that Dorothy got?

"quite a bump on her head"

100. And, finally, What is the very last thing that Dorothy says in the movie?

"Oh, Auntie em, there's no place like home!"

Part II

Judy in 1935.

Introduction

"I'd like to get something straight. I am not a tragic person. I do not cry. People are always writing that I'm bursting into tears. Well, the only thing I ever burst into is a song or a good yuck."

- Judy Garland in 1962

The following pages offer a pictorial look at the life and career of Judy Garland from her birth in 1922 until her passing in 1969. This is by no means a complete or definitive presentation of Judy's life or career. These photos are but a few highlights which serve to illustrate the genius, the talent, the love, the person who was Judy Garland.Kind and honest, funny and sincere, warm and compassionate, Judy Garland was a devoted daughter, sister, wife, friend and mother who did the best she could in all situations.She never allowed herself to be defeated, she faced life's challenges with courage and strength, she loved her children more than anything else and always tried to do the best by and for them. She will always be remembered for bringing joy to millions of people the world over.

Please note: There have been many books, documentaries and articles produced about Judy Garland.Most of these works have chosen to use photos of Judy that have been seen many times over. It has been our intention to present as many rare and unique photos of Judy as possible.To that end, a number of the photos used in this book originated in the form of old and damaged negatives or photos.They have been reproduced to the best of our ability in keeping within the restraints and guidelines of the publisher. While some photos will appear of lesser quality, it was deemed best to keep them a part of the book due to their rare and unique nature.For more information write judybook@judybook.com

Preface

Over the past thirty years, many claims have been made regarding Judy Garland. Some have reflected the audiotapes Judy made, while others have referred to the beginning notes to an autobiography from the late 1950's/early 1960's. Both of these sources have been liberally quoted in previous Garland projects dating back to the 1960's and although seemingly in Judy's own words, these works are not completely reflective of her life.

It must be noted that the brief autobiographical manuscript was filtered through at least one known ghostwriter and editor, that more than sixty-eight pages would never be completed, were never reviewed by Judy and were previously presented in edited forms and without her input. There are several different tape recordings, made over the course of several years during the 1960's, that have circulated for more than three decades. Judy did indeed record a small amount of commentary for the possibility of inclusion (after review and editing which she never did) in an autobiography. Most of the recordings, however, were made to meet her own personal needs at that time and were never intended for public consumption.

Judy recorded a little more than four hours of thoughts, most of which are devoted to warm and loving memories of her childhood, her family, her children. Predictably, it has been only those isolated and distorted expressions of inner and outer conflict that have ever been made public and without any regard or provision for at least a little perspective. Judy herself says in the tapes that she was "going through so many moods" that everything on the tapes will "have to be straightened out."

Most previous Garland projects have concentrated on the ubiquitous source who "requests anonymity" and who provides details that reflect opinion and speculation rather than fact. Additionally, there has been an almost perverse interest in what may or may not have occurred in Judy's most private moments. Judy herself never commented upon her personal actions, relationships and struggles. Many of the accounts of such have their foundation in craven, anonymous sources and several stories have been proved completely false.

It must also be remembered that Judy suffered through her greatest trials during a time when the effects of medication, prescription or otherwise, were not completely understood, nor were there available any of the support and treatment centers that are today as commonplace and accepted as fast food restaurants. As such, Judy's down periods were never presented, either at the time they were occurring or afterward, in the proper light.

In the years following Judy Garland's death, numerous books, documentaries and magazine articles have sought to provide readers with information on the beloved star. Most of this material, however, has been exaggerated and sensationalized so as to overshadow the many happy and heartwarming aspects of Judy's life and career. Much of the material and information disseminated about Judy after her passing eagerly embraced as fact all of the rumor, gossip, innuendo, speculation and personal opinion that abounded about her. Previous Garland interviews and articles were routinely misquoted. Events and circumstances were misconstrued and, sometimes, just plain changed around in order to further an image of Judy as "tragic victim," a characterization that she herself consistently denied and lampooned during her last years.

Judy herself never seemed bothered by the tragic image the press created. She would shrug her shoulders, point to herself and say, "Anything that anybody says about this star over here, you can't stop them. They like what they read, what they write. It doesn't matter what they say. That stuff is going to build on its own. That has nothing to do with me. What has to do with me is my family, my children and my life...that we love together and stay together. That other stuff...I don't try to fight it. It's a losing battle.

"They just don't want to know the truth about the real woman."

About the Author

Rita E.Piro's work on Judy Garland includes the book, *Judy Garland: The Golden Years,* an in-depth portrait of Judy's life, career and family history during the MGM years.The book includes more than 800 images, documents, letters and other archival material about the star. Piro was given access to the family records and archives of Garland's maternal relatives, providing much information and many images available for the first time. The forword was written by Margaret O'Brien and also included are full recaps of Judy's film, recording, radio and television history. See page iii for more information.

Baby Gumm c. 1931 (Milne Family Archives)

1

The Baby

It was probably inevitable that Frances Ethel Gumm would end up an entertainer - even if she hadn't yet celebrated her third birthday. Her parents were the popular and proud owners of a small Grand Rapids, Minnesota movie house known as The New Grand Theatre, where family had been presenting song and dance routines for a number of years.

So it was of no real surprise that December 26, 1924 when Baby Gumm, clad in a white net dress made by her mother and decorated by her two older sisters with sprigs of left-over Christmas holly, appeared on the stage of her family's theatre. With a cue from her mother who always provided the piano accompaniment to the stage acts, Baby burst into her own rendition of "Jingle Bells," complemented by her enthusiastic ringing of a small bell. At the close of the song, the audience thundered with applause and laughter and waited for Baby to exit the stage. She never did; at least not voluntarily.

"Well, when the music ended and it was time for me to bow out gracefully, I did nothing of the kind," explained Baby Gumm in later years, then known the world over as Judy Garland. "I started the song all over again! Mom laughed out loud, but started playing once again. Again the music ended. Again I had other ideas. And after five verses and four choruses, Daddy had to march out on the stage, pick up his little daughter and carry her into the wings amid quote - tumultuous applause- end quote! 'I wanna sing some more,' I kept protesting. I remember Daddy telling me this - 'I wanna sing some more' - and he said he was sure my voice could be heard out front long after I'd vanished, over his shoulder, into the fringe of canvas Christmas trees. I took one look at all those people, laughing and applauding, and I fell hopelessly in love with audiences. It has been a serious romance."

Left: Ethel and Frank Gumm c. 1932. (Milne Family Archives)

Francis Avent Gumm was born in Murfreesboro, Tennessee. Ethel Marion Milne was a Michigan native raised in Wisconsin. Ethel's family had been performing in local amateur productions as far back as the 18th century, while Frank had taken up entertaining as a young man. The couple met when Frank was performing as a singer in a Wisconsin moviehouse where Ethel provided the piano accompaniment. Frank and Ethel married in January 1914 and started touring as "Jack and Virginia Lee, Sweet Southern Singers." When the Gumms learned that they were to be parents, they quit their touring and settled down to living in the town of Grand Rapids, Minnesota. Their first daughter Mary Jane (called "Suzanne" or "Susie" as an adult) was born in 1915, followed by Dorothy Virginia (nicknamed Jimmie) in 1917. In late 1921, Ethel found herself pregnant for a third time. The Gumms had hoped to be able christen this child Francis Gumm, Jr., but when yet another little girl arrived, delivered on June 10, 1922, the Gumms simply changed the "i" to an "e" and named the baby "Frances Ethel" for both her parents. Said Judy as an adult, "My parents were hoping for a boy, but I don't think they were too disappointed with another girl." When Frank asked his daughters what they should call their new baby sister the girls were stumped until five year-old Jimmie offered, "Let's just call her Baby."

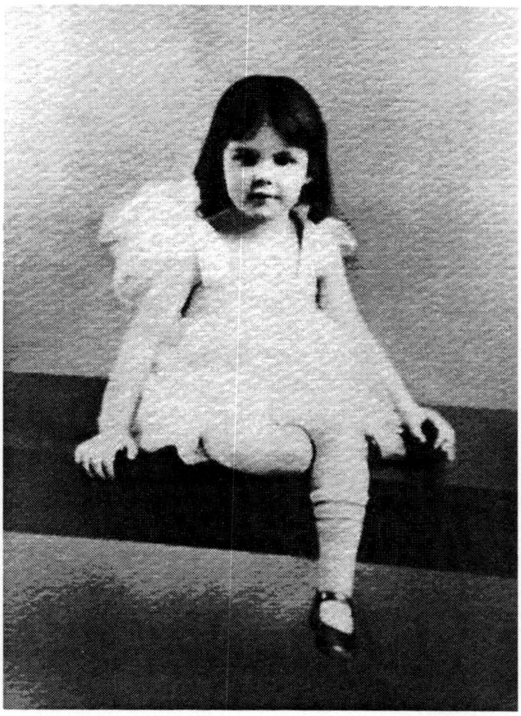

TOP Baby Gumm at age one.
Seven and five years younger than Janey and Jimmie respectively, Baby was petted, cosseted and adored by both family and friends. Said her uncle, Fred Milne, "The whole family fawned over Baby. She had some personality, and she was full of giggles. Every time you saw her she was laughing."

BOTTOM The Gumm Sisters c.1925.
The Gumm Sisters and their parents appeared in song and dance not only on the stage of the family theatre, but also in local productions in and around the Grand Rapids, Minnesota area. The family was well received by audiences and the girls loved performing as much as their parents.

Judy & Minnesota

"Everything I can remember about Grand Rapids has charm and gaiety, you know, and I remember when I - the first time I can remember singing when anybody took any notice was, my father was playing the piano, and I had a little girlfriend I don't remember her name, but she was so small, she couldn't have been more than about two, and he taught us to sing "My Country 'Tis of Thee," and he played it, and he conned my mother and sisters into listening to this little girl; and I was terribly proud because they said she was good, you know. [meaning] Baby. Baby Gumm."

"I do remember it was terribly happy.... At the very beginning, I can go back to that time, you know, and I remember my mother and father. My father owned the New Grand, a little theater in Grand Rapids. We had a lovely house and he was very successful. That had happened since he had married my mother, and when they found that they were going to have a family, they settled down in Grand Rapids, and he bought a theatre. My mother used to play the piano at the theatre, and sometimes my dad would hire someone else to play the piano for movies."

"My mother and father used to do summer stock. My mother and father were very happy there. I really remember a white dress that my mother made for me to, uh - and that was the first dress I appeared on stage in, in my father's theater. There's a picture of it. You've seen that picture of a little white sort of net dress. (see photo page 137) I can remember her making that dress. Really."

"I do remember it was terribly terribly, happy....

"I remember the snow. I remember also my grandfather and grandmother lived in Duluth. We used to take train rides, the three kids and my mother, and go visit my grandmother and grandfather. Grandmother would meet us at the train with taffy to be pulled - we'd have a taffy pull. My grandmother used to let me drink tea at her house - it was always green tea. Her name was Fitzpatrick, my mother's mother. Her (Ethel's) maiden name was Milne, but her (Grandmother) name was Fitzpatrick, Eva."

"But then sometimes in the winter, when my dad would be at the theater and my mother would be playing the piano, we would go out into the snow. I remember there was alwavs a great big can of Thompson's Malted Milk, I think was the name of it, and it was just stuff you mixed in a malt, chocolate malt. My older sister took care of those two younger sisters, and we'd go out in the snow, and we'd make angels. We'd lie down and we'd do like this, with your arms, like a bird, and you'd get up and it looks like an angel. Then we'd all go in the house and have hot milk and that Thompson's cocoa, and I just adored that."

"There was a lake, a Lake Pokegama. You know, one of those Indian names, Pokegama. We used to go there in the summertime. I can remember vaguely my father and mother taking me and the three girls to swim in Lake Pokegama. I remember one time I couldn't swim, and my oldest sister, I think it was, Mary Jane (Suzy), or Jimmy, carried me out into the water, stumbled, and dropped me, and there was a great fuss because I was scared, and I got wet, and the whole family gathered around."

"Certainly my first large, blurry memory is of music, music all the time, music all over the house. We shall have music wherever we go should have been the Gumm motto."

- Judy Garland on memories of her family

ABOVE: Baby with Henry, one of the family dogs. (Milne Family Archives)

The entire Gumm family held fond memories of Minnesota. Said Ethel, "We lived in Grand Rapids for twelve years and were very happy there." Although she could barely remember Minnesota, having left at age four, Judy would call her time there "among my happiest years." The Gumm family was active in community affairs and they were prominent members of their local Episcopal Church parish. Ethel was widely known for her hospitality, while townspeople agreed that, "There wasn't anyone who didn't like Frank Gumm."

ABOVE: Frank and Ethel with daughters, Mary Jane, 11, Jimmie, 9, and Baby, 3

The Minnesota winters were very harsh with temperatures falling well below zero in the winter along with several feet of snow through mid-April. The Gumms had several friends and family members who had made the move westward to California and its lovely promises of year-round sunshine, good economic conditions and healthy living. In mid June 1926, Mr. & Mrs. Gumm and their three daughters set out on an extended summer vacation with the ultimate destination being California where they would stay with friends in the Los Angeles area. The family took a roundabout route west by railroad, stopping in several cities along the way to perform at local theatre houses. The Gumms were so taken with the West Coast that by the time they were ready to head back to Minnesota, the decision had been made to move the family permanently to California.

California, here we come...

Much has been made of Frank and Ethel Gumm's decision to relocate from Minnesota to California. Many insist that the Gumm family was actually forced to flee Grand Rapids because of scandal stemming from Frank Gumm's rumored sexual indiscretions, but there does exist much that proves contrary to this idea.

Based entirely upon personal opinion and hearsay and surfacing in public decades after the involved members of the Gumm family were deceased, these stories have never been attributed to any real source. All of the accounts feature nondescript acts, unidentified characters or participants, and illogical sequences of time and location. No firsthand information has ever been offered and no one, male or female, adult or youth, has ever claimed to have had any type of illicit association with either Frank or Ethel Gumm. The only foundation given to statements accusing Frank Gumm of any questionable activity is based upon nondescript, fragmented, unclear stories and vague circumstances passed along by a small number of people, at least one of whom was known to have been involved in a long-standing dispute with the Gumms.

If Frank had been run out of several cities because of such repeated behavior (which was then illegal even between consenting adults), especially that involving "youth and boys," it would seem likely that there would exist some tangible evidence to uphold the accusation. As it is known, a review of state records in Tennessee, Wisconsin, Minnesota, and California, locations where Frank lived and worked, has failed to produce any record of his arrest or court appearance on any matter. (A search conducted under Frank's favored stage name of "Jack Lee" was also void.) Additionally, no single person or group of people has ever claimed to have taken part in the removal, forced or otherwise, of Frank Gumm from any town, nor is there any record (including any newspaper or police reports) of such an event ever having taken place anywhere.

The idea that the Gumm family was forced to leave Grand Rapids quickly and covertly is without foundation. Their departure was quite leisurely, spanning a period of several months' preparation, and they were the recipients of several farewell parties, including one given by their Episcopal parish church. Frank and Ethel did not sell their Grand Rapids home until after they had been settled in California for over one year so as to ensure that they would be able to return to some security in Minnesota if the move did not go well, a fact made known by Ethel before the family departed.

While some have claimed that the rumors were "common knowledge," it is unlikely that Frank Gumm would have enjoyed the popularity, prosperity and respect he did in both Grand Rapids and Lancaster, two small, provincial, working class, early twentieth century communities enveloped in a blanket of cautious, almost prudish, conservatism, had there been any truth to these rumors. The local

LEFT: The Gumm girls just before the family left for California on October 30, 1926.

newspapers of both towns were filled with almost daily accountings of the family's activities, as well as notices of praise and appreciation for their work with and contribution to both communities. Ethel never revealed any hint of any type of upsetting situation to anyone and she has never been quoted or known to have had a bad word against her husband, nor did she ever express anything but satisfaction with her marriage.

One of the Gumm family acquaintances was Marcella Rabwin, the wife of the family's very good friend and family physician, Marc Rabwin, who, along with his brother, Harry Rabwin, the Gumm family lawyer, maintained a close relationship with the Gumms. While the family was close friends with Marc and Harry, their relationship with Marcella was less pronounced. In recent years, in interviews with various tabloid media before her death in 1998, Marcella Rabwin provided completely incorrect, uncorroborated, and unsubstantiated information about Frank Gumm, information that had no foundation and whose details and timeline of events were grossly inaccurate. (It is interesting to also note that while Marcella Rabwin claimed to have been closely regard by the Gumm family, she was never able to provide information about any other Gumm family activities or involvement with them and that no one in the Gumm family ever spoke of her as being involved with them.)

Additionally, Frank Gumm spent six years at The University of the South at Sewanee, in both the prep school and college, and none of Frank's friends or teachers ever spoke of any type of scandal or less than honorable activity involving Frank Gumm.

But neither would Ethel be spared an accusatory finger of blame for the move to California. Although Judy herself (in later years, when not at her physical or emotional best) would fuel the accusations that Ethel uprooted the family in order to push her daughters into show business, numerous credible reports, including those from her older daughters, neighbors and professional connections, indicate otherwise. Ethel herself described a normal course of events leading up to the family's departure from Minnesota.

"My husband and I didn't come out to California to shove our little brood into show business," she insisted. "We were very happy in Grand Rapids, Minnesota. We'd lived there twelve years. Frank had a picture theatre and everything was going beautifully. We came to California to get away from the coal bills and the storm windows. We came to California on a family vacation and we had a wonderful time. Walked our fool heads off. Camped on the lawn of the old Warner studio on Sunset and watched the movie stars come out. Of course, we wanted to see them, just as any tourist wants to see them today.

"But what Frank and I really loved was the climate. Roses and balmy skies in the middle of winter. This was the place we decided; this was it.Back we went, sold our theatre and packed up our goods and our youngsters.Then we found on returning that most of the LA theatres were owned by the big chains - and so we finally bought a theater in the little desert town of Lancaster, and settled down."

Just as Ethel had indicated, after a few months with friends in California, Frank found a movie house in Lancaster, California in an area known as Antelope Valley, sixty miles outside of Los Angeles. In May 1927, the Gumms of Grand Rapids became the Gumms of Lancaster, owners of The Valley Theatre.

TOP Judy and sister Jimmie on a stop enroute to California in 1926.

The Gumm family arrived in California during the latter part of 1926. Frank purchased a small movie house sixty miles away from LA, in the desert town of Lancaster. Disappointed that they could not settle in the more developed and sophisticated Los Angeles area, neither Judy or Ethel ever cared much for the town. Said Ethel in 1939, "We had a big house and the school was good, but I don't know how we put up with that little sun-baked desert town for seven years," and there was always a lingering negative sentiment in Lancaster for her and for Judy, who described her Lancaster neighbors as, "as barren and dry as the desert town itself."

"We lived a terribly normal existence. There was none of that 'born in a trunk bit.' We were one very happy family."

- Jimmie Garland

ABOVE The Gumm Sisters c. 1928, as part of The Meglin Kiddies, a semi-professional troupe of child performers.

The little Gumm girls, as well as their parents, had a love of being on stage. Said eldest daughter Janey in later years, "It was great fun performing and we all enjoyed it.Judy, being the smallest, was always in the middle and she would tickle both of us in the ribs while we were singing and not crack a smile herself. She was always trying to make us laugh." Said middle daughter Jimmie, "We lived a terribly normal existence. There was none of that 'born in a trunk bit.' We were one very happy family." According to Jimmie, "The great event of Judy's childhood occurred when she sang, 'I Can't Give You Anything But Love,' at the Loew's State Theatre in LA when she was six." Judy herself described the event with much comic zeal, "Dressed as Cupid, I was to sing a solo, 'I Can't Give You Anything But Love.' Then disaster. For I awoke on the eventful morning with a cold sore, a sty on my right eye and the horrible results of my first home permanent almost totally disabling me. I couldn't see, my eye was practically shut, my mouth was swollen with the cold sore, and my hair looked like Topsy's after a pillow fight. Anyway, I showed then, for the first time, that the old, 'the show must go on,' slogan was in my bones because - a very sorry looking Cupid did the blind staggers onto the stage. I couldn't even get the quivers out of my case on account of how I couldn't see to get them out! But everyone insists I was a smash."

Frank Gumm

Frank Gumm in late 1933

• Francis Avent Gumm was born in Murfreesboro, Tennessee on March 20, 1886. He was the fourth of five children, (fours boys and one girl) of William Tecumseh Gumm & Elizabeth (Clemmie) Baugh.

• William Gumm had married into the prosperous family mercantile business of his wife. The business had branches in three southern states.

• Elizabeth Gumm was a sickly woman who passed away in 1896 at the age of 39. William Gumm was a poor businessman and lost most of the family business after his wife's death. He died in 1906.

• Young Frank possessed a rich voice and sang weekly with the church choir.

• Frank Gumm attended The University of the South, a Tennessee academic stronghold associated with the Episcopal Church. He had previously attended the school's prep academy and was well-known as a student actor/performer. Frank left college in his sophomore year, soon after his father's death, to take up performing.

• Frank supported himself as a state court reporter until 1912 when he decided to become a full-time entertainer, heading north where Vaudeville was strong. He found work as a "between films singer" at a theatre in Wisconsin. Ethel Milne was the piano accompanist at the theatre.

• Frank left Wisconsin in the fall of 1913 for a theatre engagement in Washington State. When the engagement was through, he headed back to Wisconsin where he married Ethel Milne in January 1914.

• Frank Gumm was half-owner of The New Grand Theatre in Grand Rapids, Minnesota, where he and his wife had settled down to live. He also owned partial interests in three other theatres in the Northern Minnesota area.

• Frank Gumm moved his family out to California in late October 1926, after a two month summer vacation out west that convinced the family to relocate.

• Frank had wanted to buy a theatre in Los Angeles, but could not since all the theatres in the larger cities were owned by the film studios.

• Frank settled for a small theatre in the desert town of Lancaster, 60 miles from Los Angeles in an area known as Antelope Valley.

• After seven years in Lancaster, the Gumm family moved closer to Los Angeles, purchasing a theatre in Lomita.

• Frank was well known as being quite taken with Hollywood, often waiting outside of studios to introduce himself to a favorite star or of arranging to visit a studio in order to witness firsthand its behind the scenes workings.

• A few months after opening the Lomita Theatre, Frank Gumm took seriously ill the evening of November 15th, 1935. His condition was diagnosed as pnemoniacocic meningitis. He entered into a coma and passed away on November 17, 1935.

Ethel Gumm

Judy and her mother, Ethel Gumm, in 1940

• Ethel Gumm was born Ethel Marion Milne on November 17, 1893 in Michigan. She was the second and oldest child of the seven surviving children of Evelyn and John Milne. One other childdied in infancy and another in childhood.

• The Milne Family moved to Wisconsin in 1903. Some reports have indicated that Ethel had been forced to leave school in order to help support the family, but this is untrue. Records show that John Milne was a well-paid, successful engineer for the South Shore Railroad.

• Ethel played the piano from childhood, taught music, dance and singing, and was able to compose and arrange music.

• Frank Gumm was performing as a singer in a theatre in Superior, Wisconsin when he met and fell in love with Ethel Milne, the theatre's piano accompanist. Ethel and Frank Gumm were married in January 1914 in Wisconsin.

• Ethel Gumm was known as more intelligent, articulate, hard working, unconventional and independent than other women of her day. She was a superb cook ("My mother was a helluva cook," said Judy) and coordinator/hostess of many community and church events. She was more well-liked by friends in Minnesota than in California. Ethel took three years off her age when she hit fifty and never admitted to them again.

• Ethel's mother and other Milne family members lived full-time with the Gumm family in both Minnesota and California. Ethel's youngest sister, (who outdid her older sister by taking *six* years off her own age), was a B-level entertainer, performing in bit parts in movies and in small nightclubs in Hollywood.

• MGM executives recalled Ethel's memos and notes to the studio all in an effort to make sure that Judy was content and not overburdened by studio demands. Ethel was a close friend of Ida Koverman, Louis B. Mayer's personal assistant.

• No one has ever presented or given witness to any incident of Ethel Gumm's physical, emotional or psychological mistreatment of either Judy or her sisters. While stories of other stars' mothers, including those of Shirley Temple, Jean Harlow, Jane Withers and Elizabeth Taylor, make factual note of these ladies as engaging in such classic stage mother behavior as standing behind directors giving directions to their daughter through hand signals or punishing their daughter in public for not performing on command, it is interesting to note that no one has ever presented or given witness to any incident of Ethel Gumm acting as such towards Judy or her other daughters.

• Ethel Gumm died suddenly on January 3, 1953 from a heart attack. While reports circulated of Ethel's being forced to work because Judy would not provide for her, other records, including tax forms, indicate that Judy took care of both her mother and grandmother until their deaths. Both Ethel's doctor and her lawyer insisted that Ethel worked out of a desire to keep busy and not out of necessity. Ethel lived out her last years in a home in Hollywood, purchased and maintained by Judy.

LEFT Janey 19, Jimmie 17 and Baby 12.

The Gumm sisters lived a full life in Lancaster, California.They performed occasionally in local area venues, and also made a few film shorts based upon storybook tales including *Bubbles*, *A Holiday in Storyland*, and *The Wedding of Jack and Jill.* Ethel Gumm was a devoted wife and mother who put her family first. Although she would later be falsely characterized as an exploitative and negligent mother, fact-based details, including those supplied by her daughters, describe Ethel as a loving, kind and open mother, often criticized for being too indulgent. Ethel Gumm went out of her way to make her daughters' lives as a comfortable as possible. She was known to let them sleep as late as they could, both during the school week and on weekends, bring them breakfast in bed and relieve them of any household chores. The Gumm daughters were recalled as the most well-dressed, well-mannered and well-off neighborhood children. Ethel rarely disciplined any of the girls and took much pride in the fact that she never spanked them. "I don't believe in it," she'd say. "Besides, none of my girls ever needed much discipline."

ABOVE Ethel Gumm beams proudly at her daughters in a photo taken while the group performed in Chicago in 1934.

By 1933, the Gumm family was finally able to make the move to Los Angeles where Judy was enrolled in the Lawlor School for Professional Children.The following summer of 1934, the sisters performed at the Oriental Theatre in Chicago. It was here that the sisters received the name Garland from the theatre's master of ceremonies, George Jessel. Jessel had convinced the sisters that their name was unsuitable for a show business career and, on the spur of the moment, borrowed the last name of his friend, New York newspaper writer and theatre critic, Robert Garland, and renamed the girls *The Garland Sisters.*

Ethel Gumm and her daughters at the 1934 World's Fair in Chicago.

Mother Gumm

It has been suggested that Ethel Gumm forced her daughters into performing and that she administered "pep" pills to them beginning in the late 1920's in order to keep them performing. The sisters genuinely enjoyed their time performing together, (said Judy as an adult, "No one ever forced us into performing"), and stimulants such as "pep" pills were unavailable anywhere by anyone until their first manufacture in 1937. According to the Harvard University Press, until that time, scientists were able to synthesize amphetamine only in inhalant form, and in 1932 the Benzedrine inhaler debuted, produced and marketed only as a relief for respiratory problems. Amphetamine in pill form, along with other stimulants known as "pep pills," were not available until December 1937, when Benzedrine in tablet form was introduced as a cure for numerous ailments, as well as as a weight loss aid. Until that time, amphetamine was only available by medical laboratories and was able to be introduced into the body only through injection. It is highly unlikely, if not completely impossible, that a small town housewife such as Ethel Gumm would have had either the knowledge of or the means and opportunity to obtain an experimental medicinal substance that was only just being tested by the major medical institutions and that had to be administered through injection.

None of the Gumm daughters ever spoke of being given any type of pill or food or other substance that would have produced a stimulant effect, nor did they ever speak of being given injections by their mother or by anyone else, an act that would stand out in anyone's childhood memories. Additionally, as noted as far back as their 1937 introduction, when given to children and young teens, amphetamines and stimulants have the exact *opposite* effect as that produced in adults. Amphetamines in children and young teens act as a calming agent, relaxing and quieting the child, not exciting or animating him/her. The entire issue of Ethel, her daughters and amphetamines is clearly an unreasonable one.

It has also been suggested that Ethel Gumm traded sexual favors for bookings for her girls. This is based upon pure conjecture, as there is no evidence of such activity on Ethel's part. In actuality, Ethel Gumm was far better known as being prudish rather than prurient.

Judy and her mother disembarking from the 20th Century Ltd. in Miami during the 1938 *Everybody Sing* tour.

2

The Child

The year 1935 brought a world of change to the Gumms. With Frank's purchase of a new movie house in the suburb of Lomita, the family became permanent residents of Los Angeles. As a trio the girls were performing fairly frequently in and around the Los Angeles area. Baby also appeared occasionally by herself on weekends at a few small theatres.

In mid-June, Ethel and the girls embarked on a six-week working vacation at The Cal-Neva Lodge in Lake Tahoe. At one point, the lodge manager insisted to Ethel that Baby sing for some of his special guests, one of whom, a Hollywood agent named Al Rosen, asked Ethel about representing her daughter.

Back in Los Angeles, the Gumms agreed to let Rosen represent their youngest daughter. With the September marriage of eldest sister Janey and the increasing prospect of a wedding for middle sister Jimmie, Judy was, by her own volition, now performing solo.

At this time in Hollywood, the studios eagerly looked for new talent in the form of children under the age of twelve or beautiful young women of twenty-one. Teenage stars were virtually nonexistent since the studios mistakenly believed that teenagers were not big moviegoers and almost all child stars (including, eventually, Shirley Temple) seemed to lose their appeal after they reached adolescence. It was a hard sell for Al Rosen and in later years Judy would say, "Al towed me all over, from one studio to the next. They all said the same thing. Get her away from here. There's nothing I can do with her."

"Judy was twelve when we moved to L.A., and a very normal little girl." - Jimmie Garland

TOP Judy's first MGM portrait sitting in November 1935.

At age thirteen, Baby Gumm was just plain sick of her infantile nickname and, taking her cue from the title of her then favorite song by Hoaghy Carmichael, informed her family that she was now to be known as *Judy*."At first my family continued to call me Baby, my name since infancy, but I wouldn't answer until they said Judy, In about three weeks they gave up."

Judy had two auditions with MGM studio head Louis B. Mayer and his executive staff, the first being a last minute call to the studio on September 13, 1935. Within a few days a second audition was held and, at the suggestion of Mayer's personal assistant, Mrs. Ida Koverman, Judy finished the audition with a traditional Hebrew piece, "Eli, Eli." Mrs. Koverman knew that Mayer had a soft spot for the song and, although the Gumms were not Jewish, Judy and her sisters had been taught the song by a rabbi for a special performance a few years back. The final audition proved a success and a memo to draw up a contract was sent.

"You see, I was, to the studios, no age. I wasn't a child wonder, nor was I an ingénue or a grown up. A teenager was regarded as a menace to the industry until she could be made into a glamour job. They simply didn't know what to do with me." - Judy Garland

Original caption for the above photo from November 10, 1935 press release reads: Appearing on one of Frank Fay's undiscovered stars program which holds forth at the Cafe Trocadero in Hollywood every Sunday night, is Judy Garland, juvenile torch singer who was recently signed by Louis B. Mayer of M.G.M. studios for a long term contract. Judy is being congratulated just after her appearance by, left to right, Una Merkel, Fred Keating and Spencer Tracy. One week after this performance, Judy's father, Frank Gumm, passed away suddenly from pneumococcal meningitis. Judy would always recall her father's death as "the worst event of my life." Said Ethel of the timing of Judy's contract and her husband's death, "I was glad that Judy had the studio then. At least it wasn't tied up with a million memories of her Daddy."

Judy's Screen Test

· September 13, 1935 ·

Because she was an accomplished pianist, Ethel Gumm was often asked to accompany local stage productions. Such was the case on September 13, 1935. Ethel was gone for the day, rehearsing a show for a community theatre group in Pasadena, so Frank was home alone with Judy when agent Al Rosen called. "Get Judy down to MGM immediately," he told Frank Gumm. "I've made an appointment and they're waiting to hear her."

Judy, who had been tending to some garden chores and playing in the dirt with her Pekingese pup, Phooey, was in no condition to be brought to an audition. Dressed in dirty slacks, sneakers and a play shirt, Judy asked if she had to change her clothes. "No," said Frank, "they'll like you as you are."

Judy and Frank were ushered into the office of Louis B. Mayer, the head of Metro-Goldwyn-Mayer, known as MGM, the biggest and most important movie studio in the world. Mr. Mayer's special assistant, Mrs. Ida Koverman (Mrs."Kay") always handled the first part of an audition and she was extremely influential with the MGM boss. (Koverman had been personally recommended to Mayer by former President Herbert Hoover for whom she had also worked as a personal assistant during his administration. Throughout her life, Koverman maintained close social and professional ties with Washington and the White House.)

Frank sat down at the piano and Judy began to sing. Frank was not a pianist and neither he nor Judy were at their best. Mrs. Koverman sent for Roger Edens, MGM's newest music arranger and accompanist. With Roger at the keyboard now, Judy sang perfectly, prompting Mrs. Koverman to send for Mr. Mayer. The MGM head, an authoritarian figure who never displayed any emotion at or reaction to an audition, listened stone-face. When he began to question and pressure Judy for more,

Frank, clearly annoyed, declared that they all had heard enough, took his child by the hand and left. He was certain they were just taking up his and his daughter's time.

Upon learning of the day's events, Ethel agreed with her husband's assessment of the experience, in fact the only thing that upset her was that Judy had left the house dressed in such an embarrassing state. "When I returned home from Pasadena," Ethel later said, "and they had told me where they'd been, I took one look at my dirt-covered child and shouted, 'You left the house looking like that!' 'Oh, what's the difference?" said Frank. "No one was impressed.'

"Believe me, we didn't care about the audition. Expecting nothing, how can you be disappointed? All I cared about was the fact that people had seen my daughter in such a state. When the unexpected happened and they called about a contract, our reaction was: 'Judy? Do you have the right little girl?'"

One more audition was called for within a few days for Mr. Mayer, Mrs. Koverman and other MGM executives. This time, however, Ethel brought Judy, making certain she was dressed more appropriately. Judy sang several songs and, at the suggestion of Mrs. Koverman, she finished the audition with a traditional Hebrew piece, *Eli, Eli*. Mrs. Koverman knew that Mr. Mayer had a soft spot for the song and, although the Gumms were not Jewish, Judy and her sisters had been taught the song by a rabbi for a special performance a few years back. The final audition proved a success and a memo to draw up a contract was sent the very same day. (There is some evidence that Judy had actually unsuccessfully auditioned previously for MGM, in a location outside of the studio, however, this account has long been the accepted record of events.)

"What do you know...Baby's been picked up by the MGM studio!"

- Frank Gumm in a 1935 letter to a friend in Grand Rapids

"I stayed at MGM and Deanna went to Universal, where they made monster movies." - Judy Garland

TOP December 30, 1935. Judy's first publicity photo with fellow child stars, Mickey Rooney and Jane Withers. Mickey Rooney and Judy Garland enjoyed each other's friendship from their earliest days together at MGM.

BOTTOM Deanna Durbin, Jackie Cooper and Judy in early 1936.

Garland & Durbin

Just prior to Judy's arrival to MGM, the studio had signed another child singer to its roster, Edna Mae Durbin. In contrast to Judy's "swing" style, Edna Mae was an operatic soprano.

Said to have been a way to decide which child singer to keep and which to let go, MGM filmed *Every Sunday*, a short test film highlighting both girls' musical abilities. Universal Studios had also seen the two girls perform, (probably at an exhibitor's presentation of *Every Sunday* since the film was not released to the public until decades later), and, taking a liking to Judy's "hot" singing style, asked for her loan out for a role in their upcoming movie *Three Smart Girls*. MGM refused.

Learning that Edna Mae's contract had lapsed and that MGM was either delaying in giving her a new one or had simply forgotten to renew her option, Universal quickly offered the little opera singer a new contract, gave her the name "Deanna" and changed the music of *Three Smart Girls* from swing to opera. *Three Smart Girls* was a tremendous hit and Deanna Durbin, an overnight success.

Although it would be a little while longer before MGM would realize the gift they had in the young Judy Garland, once they did she quickly surpassed Durbin in popularity. This was due mainly to the fact that MGM was able to develop far more spectacular musical productions than Universal, known primarily for it monster and horror movies, could ever dream of, and also because Judy's vocal concentration was on the more popular swing and standards of the time.Nevertheless, Durbin (who retired from films and singing in 1946) enjoyed an enormous popularity and single-handedly saved Universal Studios from bankruptcy. She lives today in Paris, appearing seldom, if ever, in public.She has never granted an interview or appeared in public as an actress or singer for many decades.

TOP January 11, 1936. Bonita Granville, Judy, and Betty Jaynes.

BOTTOM Rear: Bonita and Judy, front, Tommy Kelley and Sybil Jason

Judy displays a passion for party blowers in these two photos snapped at MGM sponsored affairs.Bonita Granville made numerous movies and starred in the original "Nancy Drew" film series, while Betty Jaynes appeared in numerous supporting roles for MGM.

TOP February 1937.
Although MGM considered her for a few small roles, as well as for a loan out to Hal Roach Studios for one of the "Our Gang Follies" comedies (it never materialized), Judy spent the first years of her studio contract going to school and performing at studio events. Judy's first radio appearances were with Wallace Beery on NBC's "Shell Chateau Hour" in October and November 1935. She later became a regular on CBS's "Jack Oakie College" in early 1937.

MIDDLE Fall 1935
Judy (far right) and other child actors at the MGM schoolhouse with their teacher, Mary McDonald. Judy left the MGM school in December in order to attend her local public school with her neighborhood girlfriends.

BOTTOM Spring, 1937.
Judy with Suzanne Farrell, Betty Jaynes, John Arlington, Freddie Bartholomew, and Mickey Rooney on an MGM sponsored trip to the Venice Pier Amusement Park.

Nothing was ever the same for Judy after she sang "Dear Mr. Gable/You Made Me Love You" at the February 1, 1937 studio birthday party for the then "King (note the crown on the cake) of Motion Pictures." As Judy finished the last notes of the song, the guests rose to their feet in applause and cheers. So touched was Gable that he actually cried as he took Judy in his arms. Studio executives were so taken with Judy that a part for her was ordered added to *Broadway Melody of 1938*, the studio's next big release then being filmed. Judy's film rendition of "Dear Mr. Gable" was brief, but it was the catalyst for her MGM movie career. Clark Gable never forgot Judy, or her rendition of "Dear Mr. Gable," which went on to become one of her most famous songs. Contrary to some reports, neither star ever expressed any negative sentiment for the song, and Judy was called upon to repeat the song numerous times during her years at MGM. Judy herself said of the song, "It started me on my real screen career."

TOP September 1937. Mickey celebrates his birthday on the set of *Thoroughbreds Don't Cry* with Sophie Tucker, Judy and Ronald Sinclair.

MIDDLE November 1937. *Everybody Sing* publicity still with Allan Jones, Lynn Carver and Reginald Gardner.

BOTTOM August 1938. On the set of *Listen Darling.*

By the end of 1937, Judy had completed three feature films, appearing first in *Pigskin Parade* on a loan out to 20th Century Fox in 1936. She then made *Broadway Melody of 1938, Thoroughbreds Don't Cry,* and *Silent Night*, a holiday short, all in rapid succession for MGM. By the end of 1938 she had completed *Everybody Sing*, *Love Finds Andy Hardy* (her first of three guest star appearances in the "Andy Hardy" series) and *Listen, Darling*.

TOP and BOTTOM January 27, 1938

Upon the completion of *Everybody Sing* in mid-January 1938, MGM sent Judy, with her mother and studio musical director, Roger Edens, on a publicity tour of Loew's State Theatres. Miami, Florida was the first stop on the *Everybody Sing* publicity tour. Judy appeared at at Miami Beach High School where she did a live radio braodcast and was mobbed by students.

BOTTOM Judy modeled some teen fashions for newspapers at the Roney Plaza Cabana Sun Club.

TOP & MIDDLE Arriving in New York City's Grand Central Station on February 8, 1938, Judy, accompanied by Roger Edens, offers a song with a group of Grand Central Stations porters, then known as "Red Caps" because of their distinctively-colored head gear. Roger Edens would remain Judy's musical director throughout her career with MGM.

BOTTOM In between performances Judy took lessons with a studio supplied tutor three hours a day. Here she gladly obliges a photographer. Judy is seen in this photo wearing the cross that her parents gave her for her 13th birthday. Said Judy during an interview a few years later, "No matter how many jewels I may have, I'll always remember the little cross Mom and Daddy gave me for my 13th birthday. It was the last present I ever got from my Dad before he died."

IN OLD CHICAGO
Camels
ASTOR THEATRE
IN OLD CHICAGO

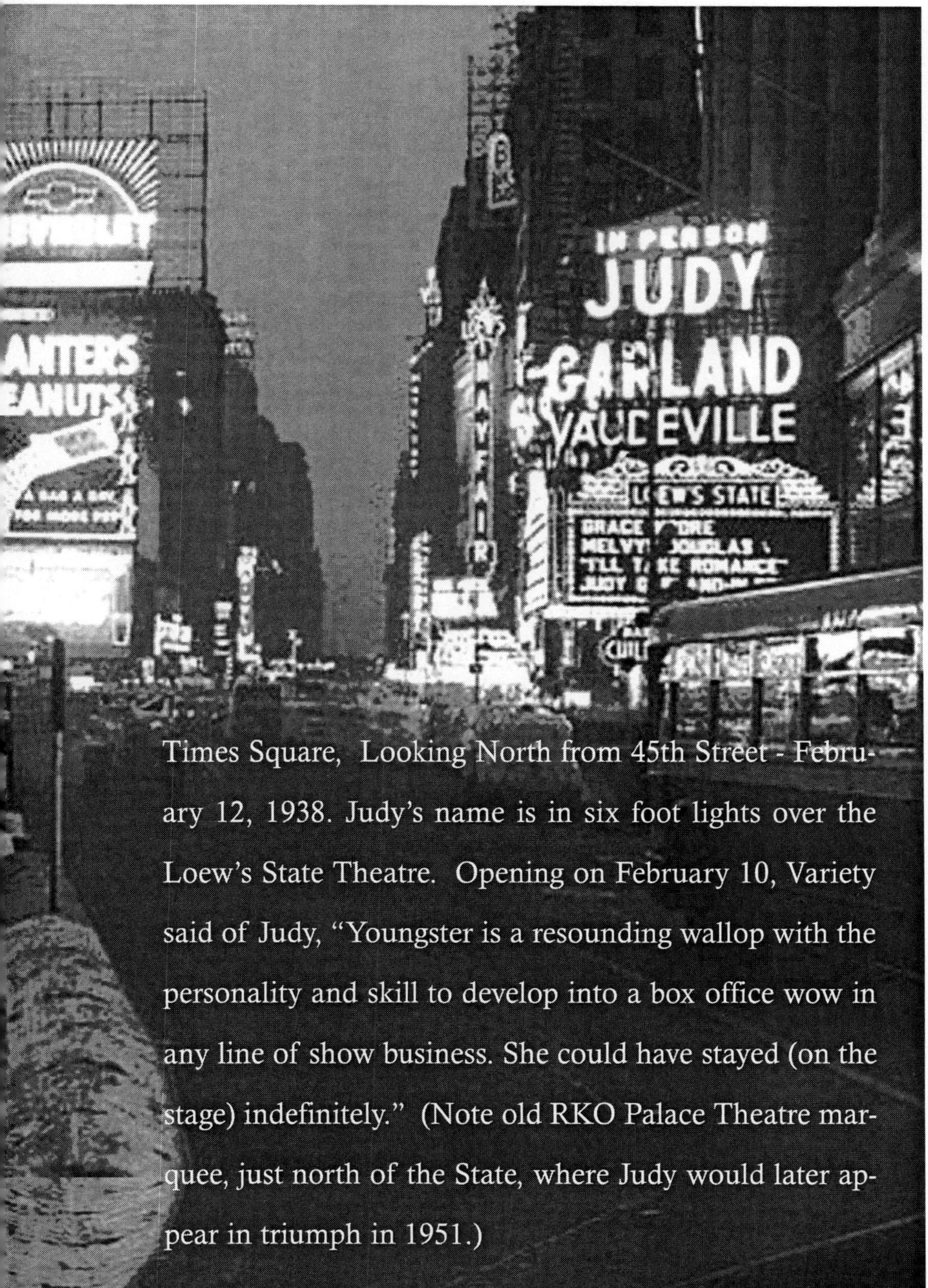

Times Square, Looking North from 45th Street - February 12, 1938. Judy's name is in six foot lights over the Loew's State Theatre. Opening on February 10, Variety said of Judy, "Youngster is a resounding wallop with the personality and skill to develop into a box office wow in any line of show business. She could have stayed (on the stage) indefinitely." (Note old RKO Palace Theatre marquee, just north of the State, where Judy would later appear in triumph in 1951.)

Judy in a 1940 publicity still. Judy's adult front teeth had grown in slightly crooked causing MGM to create a cosmetic dental appliance that she could take on and off at will. Judy was never photographed without the plate during her youth, although some photos from her post-MGM years do picture her without the cosmetic plate, revealing her natural smile.

3

The Darling

Soon after the opening of *The Wizard of Oz* in August 1939, Judy found her popularity growing in leaps and bounds. By late September of that year, Judy was receiving more fan mail than any other MGM star. (It is no small coincidence that, according to government records, the name "Judy" first became popular in late 1939, garnering the number ten spot on the list of top ten names for newborn girls for that year, followed by the number three spot for the year 1940. "Judy" remained in the top ten list through 1947.)

Had celebrity merchandising and product endorsement been well-developed at the time when the teenage Judy Garland was skyrocketing to fame, the result would have been mind-boggling. Still, companies did manage to create a huge Judy Garland novelty market. The Ideal Toy Company produced the first Judy Garland doll, modeled after "Dorothy," in late 1939 and the "Teen Judy" doll," also by Ideal, debuted in 1940. Clothing manufacturers developed a line of Judy Garland teen and pre-teen dresses and accessories. Judy Garland paper dolls, coloring books, vanity sets, school supplies and other items were all successful. Judy would begin her product endorsement career featured in several ad campaigns for CERTO gelatin, Studebaker cars, Maxwell House coffee, Lux soap and Anderson flatware.

Concerning her youth, Judy herself would say, "Although I associated with many older and wise people, and learned much from them, I was still young and basically the same as any other teenage girl." This statement was particularly true for Judy who, no matter how big a star she became, was always known for her common touch.

"It was never a case of Mama saying (of the studio) 'You do whatever they say.' Mama wanted Judy to have whatever Judy wanted. If Judy complained, then Mama went right up to the studio and complained." - Jimmie Garland

TOP & BOTTOM Judy and her mother

Contrary to popular myth, Judy and her mother shared a close, supportive and loving relationship through the mid-to-late 1940's. Many believe that Ethel Gumm eagerly carried out every MGM dictum concerning her daughter, but just the opposite is true. She often fought against the studio's overburdening demands on Judy, making her a formidable force with which L.B. Mayer had to contend. MGM employees would recall numerous letters from Ethel to studio executives filed to make sure that Judy was content and not overburdened by studio demands.

"My mother was a strong-minded woman, but she was never a 'stage mamma.'" - Judy Garland in 1951

TOP Judy and her sisters, Jimmie (r) and Susie in 1938.

Judy and her sisters shared a close relationship, and Judy never had a bad word to say about either of them. Judy often painted a two-sided picture of her childhood saying, on the one hand, that she had been "pushed" and "dragged" onto the stage and, on the other, declaring, "My sisters and I shared a wonderful childhood, performing and touring together as a family. We would play hide and seek and tag in the back part of the theatres." Said Judy in later years of her mother, "My mother was a strong-minded woman, but she was never a 'stage mamma.' Sometimes, while standing in the wings waiting to go on, we would hear mothers threatening their children, saying things like, 'You go out there or I'll break your head.' It would make us sick since we experienced none of that. No one ever talked to us like that or forced us to do anything. We were always loved and well cared for by both our parents." It is interesting to note that while Ethel Gumm has always been the most maligned character in the Judy Garland story, no one has ever described or given witness to any fact-based instance of Ethel's physical, emotional or psychological mistreatment of either Judy or her sisters.

Sister, Sister

Judy held a younger sister's adoration of and respect for her two big sisters and never had an unkind word to say about either of them. Said Jimmie Garland, "We were so close. Judy had a funny way of talking about us as if we were one person. 'Can we have some juice? *Our* throat hurts,' she'd say."

• Susie was the eldest Garland sister, born September 24, 1915. Susie's birth name was Mary Jane, after both her father's eldest sister and a great-aunt.

• At age 19, Mary Jane announced that she was discarding her birth name in favor of the more glamorous-sounding Suzanne or Susie. Soon after, little sister Frances announced her name change to Judy. Jimmie always recalled the family's mild frustration when neither daughter would answer to her birth name. Both nicknames stuck, however, and neither girl used her birth name unless for legal purposes.

• In September 1935, Sue married musician Lee Kahn whom she had met during the Gumm Sisters' six week engagement at the Cal-Neva Lodge that summer. The marriage ended in late 1937 with Sue returning to live with her mother and sisters.

• Sue was considered the best dancer among the sisters and worked intermittently as an assistant dance instructor for MGM. She also appeared in small roles in a few MGM films, as well as on radio productions of MGM films.

• Sue married Jack Cathcart in 1943. During her adult years Sue suffered through serious chronic illness including several miscarriages, along with her husband's frequent infidelities and alcoholic binges.Susie Garland passed away in early May 1964. It was initially reported that, upon learning her husband had left her for another woman, and having become increasingly despondent over her growing ill health, Sue had taken an overdose of sleeping pills. A later investigation determined that she had actually passed away from a toxic reaction to an experimental medication prescribed to her two weeks previous for a serious blood abnormality.

• Jimmie Garland was born July 4, 1917 and named Dorothy Virginia in honor of her mother's older sister who had passed away in childhood.

• Jimmie married musician/bandleader Bobby Sherwood in February 1937 (she would be his second of nine wives) and filed for divorce from him in August of that same year. Jimmie delayed the divorce after she learned that she was pregnant. The couple separated in 1941 and was divorced in 1943. Bobby Sherwood never supported his daughter and never saw her during her childhood and teen years. According to family, some of the best known rumors concerning the Garland family were begun by Sherwood.

• Jimmie's daughter was born in May 1938 and named Judith Gale in honor of her aunt. The family had intended to name the baby Judaline, since they did not want to confuse the two Judy's, ("Juda-line" was suggested by a family member who had named their daughter "Carol-ine") but their priest refused to baptize her without a Christian name. Always known as such, Judaline legally changed her name at age eighteen.

• Jimmie worked for MGM as a script girl until 1945 when she began her own singing career, appearing at several NYC and LA nightclubs. Jimmie married John Thompson in 1948.They moved to Texas in 1949. Jimmie passed away in 1977 from heart disease.

"My sisters & I shared a wonderful chidlhood...we were always loved and well-cared for by both our parents." - Judy Garland

THIS PAGE Judy at home.

Until Judy reached the then legal age of twenty-one, Ethel was responsible for all of her financial and legal concerns. Contrary to reports that she simply spent all of Judy's money, Ethel was, in actuality, a conservative financial planner. According to middle daughter Jimmie, immediately after signing the MGM contract, Ethel employed a financial firm to set up an investment plan to secure Judy's future. Said Jimmie, "Judy hired some business manager (in the later 1940's) who cashed in all of Mama's wonderful investments. After that it was one financial mess after another for Judy." Judy did, however, support her mother and grandmother, as well as claim them as tax dependents, until their deaths.

TOP and BOTTOM Judy in the Bel Air home she shared with her family.

Judy lived with her family, which included her mother, her maternal grandmother, Eva Milne, and, at various times, one or both of her older sisters and her niece in a custom designed home built in 1939 in the then newly developing area of Bel Air. The house sat on two acres with a terraced backyard and garden and a huge swimming pool, as well as a game room, miniature bowling alley, sound proof music and dance room and a badminton court. Judy had a suite of three rooms and there was space enough to accommodate the entire family, including even the family dogs who had their own multi-room doghouse.

TOP Judy with Bonita Granville and Billy Hallop.

BOTTOM (l to r,) Sidney Fields, Judy, Helen Parrish, Lois Ransom, Jackie Cooper and Bonita Granville.

TOP Judy hosts an egg hunt at her home for Easter 1939.

BOTTOM Judy, Jackie Cooper and Bonita Granville in late 1939.

More than that of any other Hollywood film family, the Garland home was the scene of many parties. Magazines loved to highlight the various events hosted by the Garlands which included Easter egg hunts, cast parties, bowling breakfasts and moonlight swim parties. Never known as a Hollywood snob, Judy also maintained close contacts with several friends outside of the studio. One childhood friend in particular recalled Judy's sense of friendship. At age ten, Judy had made a childhood promise to her then favorite girlfriend, Marjorie Ruth Wright, to sing at the youngster's wedding when they were both grown. In 1942, Marjorie was living near Judy in LA and contacted her one time playmate about her upcoming wedding. Judy called the bride saying, "Didn't I promise you something when we were ten?" Replied Marjorie, "I was hoping that you would remember!" Without a moment's hesitation, Judy arranged to be at the LA church ceremony where she sang, "Oh Promise Me," for the happy couple.

"Mickey was tough, generous, gifted and loyal. We have had a good, solid relationship over the years, not - to the disappointment of moviegoers, I guess, - in any way romantic. Professionally and as a person, he respected me, and I him."

- Judy Garland in 1951

LEFT TOP Judy and Mickey motor to the premiere of *Babes in Arms* in Mickey's station wagon.

BOTTOM The stars pose with their mothers at Grauman's Chinese Theatre.

THIS PAGE Arriving at Grauman's Chinese Theatre.

Coming on the heels of the spectacular Capitol Theatre premiere of *The Wizard of Oz* was an invitation from Mr. Sidney Patrick Grauman for Judy to add her foot and handprints to the courtyard of his famous theatre. Just after finishing *Oz*, Judy began filming another Rooney-Garland offering called *Babes in Arms*. The film did not take long to complete and was premiered in Hollywood on October 10, 1939.

TOP and BOTTOM Judy cements her fame.

It was at the Grauman's Chinese Theatre premiere of *Babes In Arms* that Judy would cast both her signature and her stardom in cement. With Mickey and her mother by her side, Judy offered, "For Mr. Grauman, All Happiness, Judy Garland," as her immortalized message set above her petite hand and footprints. Said Judy years later, "When Mickey and I made *Babes in Arms*, I got my first long dress, white and bouffant. It was for the premiere of the movie when I made my foot and handprints at Grauman's Chinese Theatre. It was all so thrilling."

TOP and BOTTOM February 29, 1940.

At age seventeen, Judy was awarded her first and only Academy Award for "Outstanding Screen Contribution by a Juvenile." Some have spoken of this honor as being somewhat of a slight against Judy, who many believe was deserving of a full "Best Actress" award for her efforts in *The Wizard of Oz*. It should be remembered that during this period, actors and actresses under the age of eighteen were only given special Juvenile Oscars. (Other "juvenile" recipients included Deanna Durbin, Mickey Rooney and Margaret O'Brien. The last recipient was Hayley Mills.) It is clear from the archival footage of the event that Judy was elated with the award, later dubbing the miniature statuette her "Munchkin Award."

"Although I associated with many older and wise people, and learned much from them, I was still young and basically the same as any other teenage girl."

- Judy Garland

LEFT TOP Judy with Dorothy Lamour and Bob Hope.

BOTTOM Judy, Bob and Jerry were a huge hit on radio.

THIS PAGE Judy, Jerry and Bob. Judy was a very welcome guest on radio shows throughout her fifteen year career with MGM. During 1938 and 1939, Judy appeared on the "Good News Show," "Leo is on The Air," "Screen Guild Theatre," "Maxwell House Coffee Time," as well as on many special event broadcasts.

"I grew to love Judy so much that her mother would wait for her after every show."

-Bob Hope

Beginning in September 1939, Judy became a regular on Bob Hope's very popular "The Pepsodent Show." Judy and Bob, along with Jerry Colonna and musical director, Skinnay Ennis, were welcome radio guests in the homes of Americans each week. During each show, Judy and Bob would engage in some gentle ribbing of one another, with Judy usually getting the most laughs at Bob's expense. Judy would then offer two or three songs, often selected according to the seasons, holidays or to highlight a new composition. Between September 1939 and May 1940, Judy completed more than twenty-five broadcasts with Hope.

In all, Judy's radio work between late 1939 and mid-1940 totaled more than forty programs, including an appearance at the grand opening of the then spectacular Arrowhead Springs Lake Resort. At this time, radio versions of movies were popular and Judy also completed several of these with Mickey, as well as with other stars. In addition to her film work, Judy had rehearsals for radio shows one or two afternoons a week. After 1940, Judy was not permitted by MGM to appear as a regular on any one radio show, this in an effort to make her broadcasts more of a special event.

"My mother loved Mr. Mayer till the end of her life...she never blamed him for what had happened to her."

- Lorna Luft

TOP Judy and MGM boss Louis B. Mayer and Jimmy Stewart in 1940.

It has often been said that Louis B. Mayer exercised a despotic, mean spirited, non-caring sentiment for Judy. This is untrue and Judy herself never made those claims, rather the characterization was made by others.There were definite negative factors associated with MGM and Louis B. Mayer, but Judy harbored no anger or resentment against either the man or his studio, and was quick to point out in a 1968 interview that, "MGM was the greatest part of my career. They made us what we are. There were lots of good times, too." One report puts L. B. Mayer at making an inappropriate advance towards the teenage Garland. This story was never offered by Judy herself, but rather was presented by a writer and appeared in a brief, unpublished work referenced only after her death. (No child or teenage star has ever accused Mayer of any such act.) Wrote daughter Lorna Luft in her memoir that, "My mother loved Mr. Mayer till the end of her life...she never blamed him for what had happened to her. She always spoke lovingly of him to us children."

TOP March 11 1940. Judy serves refreshments to two LAPD detectives called to the Garland home to protect the young singer after it was discovered that she was the object of a kidnapping plot that was quickly foiled by police.

BOTTOM Always generous with her autograph and never known to turn anyone away, Judy, with Jackie Cooper, stops to add her signature to a few fans' autograph albums. By late 1939, Judy was receiving more fan mail than any other star on the MGM lot.

TOP Judy and Fanny Brice in a 1939 radio broadcast. Brice and Judy starred in *Everybody Sing*.

BOTTOM Helen Parrish, Forrest Tucker, Judy and Ann Rutherford at a bowling party hosted by Judy in September 1939.

TOP May 1940 Judy takes part in a charity tennis match along with actress Paulette Goddard, tennis greats, Bill Tilden, Lester Stoefen and, acting as scorekeeper, Douglas Fairbanks, Jr.

BOTTOM Judy joins with First Lady Eleanor Roosevelt at a Greek War relief benefit in 1940.

TOP Judy in a publicity still set in the MGM schoolhouse.
BOTTOM Judy and her mother examine her diploma at her June 1940 high school graduation ceremony.

Once she was signed by MGM, Judy attended school on the studio lot. The MGM school was a one room schoolhouse in which the studio's youngest actors were all taught at their individual grade levels. Judy never cared for the studio school and asked to attend the local public school with her neighborhood friends. Judy attended regular classes at her local public school for about a year. Once she began making films on a regular basis, she could no longer attend public school and was tutored privately in her dressing room. Judy graduated from University High School on June 28, 1940 in a ceremony that, by Judy's request, barred press photographers from entering inside the school building. Judy was one of the few child stars of the time to actually attend her graduation ceremony.

TOP Judy's favorite teenage portrait sitting done for her 18th birthday in June 1940.

Although she could never be classified as overweight, MGM never made secret that it was not fond of young Judy's figure. Almost from day one of her contract, studio heads tried to get Judy to follow a stringent reducing diet. What is not true is that her mother played a part in any of this. Numerous sources clearly indicate Ethel's opposition to MGM's dietary restrictions for her daughter, and it would be her maternal instincts that, in spite of MGM's desires, would maintain Judy's fuller teen figure. "While young Judy starved at the studio, her mother just continued to feed her up at home," wrote one reporter in 1943. As related by sister Jimmie Garland, administering pills to Judy in order to cut her appetite was discussed with Ethel who, unfamiliar as everyone else with the new drug's side effects, agreed to try them out in mid-1938. But after a just a few days use, with Judy experiencing only discomfort with no change in her eating patterns, Ethel refused to continue giving them to her daughter. Judy's somewhat fuller - and healthier - figure would remain clearly evident in her photos and films through 1941. While she may not have been considered a "glamour girl" by MGM standards, Judy was still very attractive, especially after she entered her late teens. But you could not convince Judy that she possessed even the slightest of good looks. "Tis not my beauty that draws them to my pictures, let's be frank about that" she told an interviewer. "I may sing and dance and do a halfway decent job at acting, but beauty? Not me."

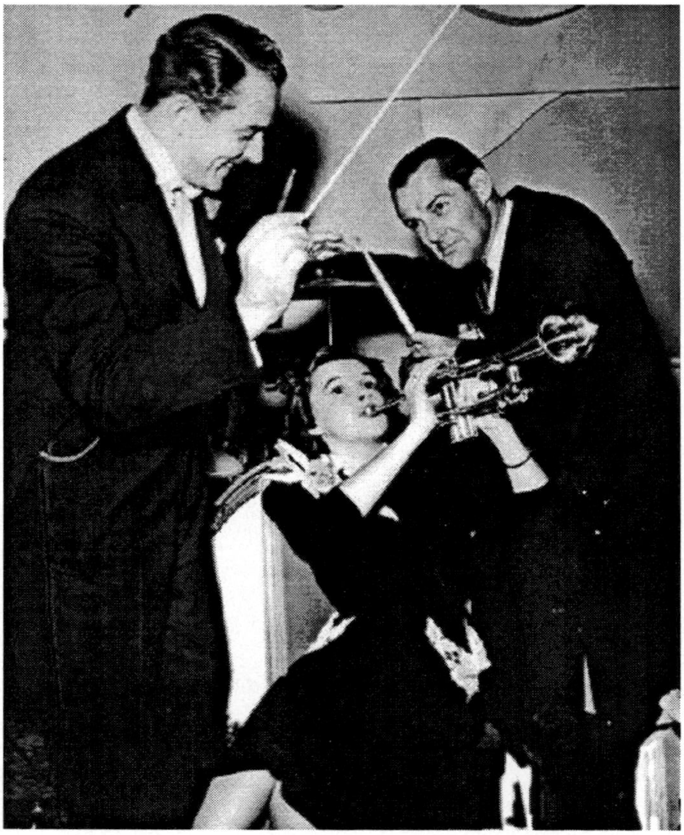

TOP Bandleader Glen Gray, Judy and Hollywood columnist Jimmy Fidler clown around in a 1940 jam session in the Palm Court of the Palace Hotel in San Francisco, California.

BOTTOM Judy confers on a music matter with, at left, conductor George Stoll and, at right, Roger Edens.

TOP Spring 1940.
Judy at Warner's Hollywood Theatre with actress Margaret Sullavan, wife of agent Leland Hayward, who negotiated Judy's 1940 MGM contract of $2000 per week. (Equal today to about $25,000 per week.) After the success of *The Wizard of Oz*, MGM tore up Judy's original 1935 contract (with more than two years remaining at $500 per week) and offered her a new and more lucrative agreement.

TOP June 1940 At her 18th studio birthday party, held in the MGM Executive Dining Room, Louis B. Mayer presents Judy with a personal sized studio recording machine. Soon after turning eighteen, Judy began to bristle at always being portrayed as a "little girl" in films. MGM was seemingly bent on keeping her in a sort of perpetual adolescence. Yet, her growing beauty and blossoming figure could not be overlooked for long. Wrote one magazine reporter in 1940, "There's no denying that the Garland gal is turning into one delectable eyeful." The studio responded by casting Judy in two more mature starring roles in the films, *Little Nellie Kelly* and *Ziegfeld Girl*.

Judy relaxes on the set of *Little Nellie Kelly* with (top) her mom, Ethel Gumm, and (bottom) producer Arthur Freed and co-stars Douglas McPhail (c.) and George Murphy. While the film did not receive a tremendous ovation, Judy drew critical acclaim for her successful transition from child to at least somewhat of an adult role. *Little Nellie Kelly* provided Judy with her one and only on screen death scene which was so sensitively portrayed that the film crew was not allowed on the set during filming so as not to have their sniffles and sobs picked up by the microphones.*Little Nellie Kelly* may best be remembered, however, for the introduction of Roger Edens' composition "It's a Great Day for The Irish," which would go on to become one of the most popular of all Irish anthems.

Judy on the set of *Ziegfeld Girl* with co-stars Lana Turner and Hedy Lamaar and in her dressing room, giving her poodle Chou-Chou a comb. Some have said that "Judy wanted to be Lana Turner," but this is not entirely true. Lana was always depicted as a sophisticated glamour girl, while Judy was always posed as "the girl next door." Judy may have desired a few more sophisticated, glamorous roles, but she was ultimately very happy with and proud of her movie work. Lana always recalled Judy in the most affectionate of terms and often called her, "the greatest talent." Reports of catty animosity between the two stars is untrue and the two women shared a lifelong friendship, including raising their families together during the 1950's. Turner's daughter always recalled the two ladies' friendship in the warmest of terms.

Judy Merchandising

Judy merchandising took the form of many items including paint and paper doll books, adventure books for girls, dixie cup lids, stickers, school supplies, dolls, accessories and much more. In 1939, The Ideal Toy Company produced the first type of Judy Garland doll. The character portrayed by the doll was, of course, "Dorothy," and she came in three sizes and dressed in either a red or blue checked jumper over a white blouse. In 1940, the Ideal company introduced the "Teen Judy Doll," which was available with a trunk full of clothes. Judy did a series of publicity shots with the doll and also autographed photos which were inserted into the doll boxes. The Los Angeles Examiner ran a promotion featuring a free Judy Garland doll with every purchase of two half year subscriptions which cost the subscriber a whopping sixty cents for each!

Judy Garland merchandising included coloring books, paper dolls, clothing, accessories, school supplies, magazines, records and more.

Miss Judy Garland 1943

4

The Beauty

Always the romantic, dreamy type, Judy went from crush to crush, heartthrob to heartthrob. The main object of Judy's teenage yearning, however, was not to be a boy of merely adolescent years, but rather a twice-divorced older man.

Artie Shaw was one of the most popular bandleaders during the Swing era. Shaw never knew that Judy was in love with him. Judy pursued their relationship with phone calls and meetings, but it was clear, at least to Shaw, that it was all a purely platonic friendship. Shaw has always denied any romantic or intimate involvement with Judy and according to the former bandleader, he looked upon Judy as a kind of kid sister and nothing more.

Many believe that Judy and Shaw carried on a lengthy secret romance, but this is untrue. The press knew of Judy's infatuation with Shaw and reported regularly on their activities together as late as Christmas 1939. Although Ethel had allowed Judy to see Shaw in public and at often chaperoned events, soon after the beginning of 1940 she instructed her daughter that she was not to see the bandleader anymore. This prompted Judy to enlist the aid of several close to her in order to meet Shaw without her mother's knowledge. The meetings, however, were not to last for very long.

Artie Shaw and Lana Turner eloped the morning of February 13, 1940 after just one meeting. Judy awoke to read the news in the daily paper along with millions of other Americans. A torrent of tears and near hysteria followed the entire day with her mother and sisters all trying their best to comfort Judy. Her heartbreak over Shaw was painful and soon Judy would seek comfort in another relationship that, while temporarily soothing her pain, would serve to create even more.

TOP December 1940. Judy and David Rose bump into Jackie Cooper and Bonita Granville on the dance floor.

BOTTOM January 1941. Dave threatens Judy with a dousing of soda spray.

One evening soon after her heartache over Artie Shaw, Judy was in her dressing room waiting to go on the air when David Rose stopped by, a slice of homemade cake in hand to lift Judy's spirits. Said Judy, "I thought he was the sweetest person ever." So began their friendship, which soon blossomed into a courtship, one that was looked upon with favor only by its two participants. Rose was a British-born, soon-to-be divorced (his first marriage was to comedienne Martha Raye), thirty-one year-old musician. Though talented, he was unpopular in Hollywood, due mainly to his self-absorbed, aloof and generally dull nature. MGM tried hard to ignore the romance as did Judy's friends and family, but in the end their disapproval mattered little.

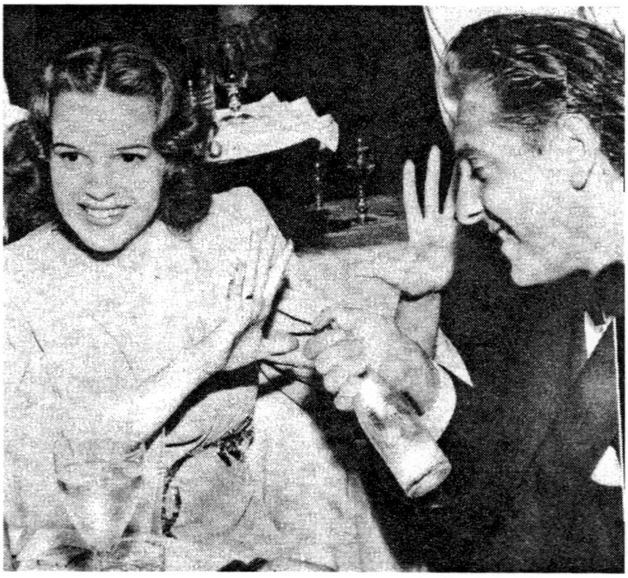

TOP Judy and Ethel at the 1941 MGM Movie Mothers Dinner.

Although Ethel Gumm was not in favor of her daughter's romance with David Rose, she knew that it was futile to try to stop it and allowed Judy to become engaged on May 27, 1941. Said Ethel, "Even if she has only one year of happiness, it is what she wants. I won't stop it."

BOTTOM Judy and Dave's engagement portrait in the yard of the Garland home.

Needless to say, news of the Garland-Rose engagement was not welcome at MGM and studio executives demanded to know how Ethel could possibly have allowed this to take place. As always, Ethel immediately sided with Judy, informing the studio that she stood by Judy's decision to marry whom and when she pleased.

TOP Judy and Dave at their engagement party with Tony Martin and Lana Turner

BOTTOM The newly-engaged couple cut their 40-lb heart-shaped cake

The formal engagement of Judy Garland to David Rose was announced at a garden party held at the Garland home on June 15, 1941, during which Dave presented Judy with a four carat square-cut diamond ring. Though they had indicated that they intended to marry later in 1941, Judy and Dave surprised all of Hollywood by being married five weeks after their engagement in a Las Vegas ceremony. Ethel accompanied her daughter to the nuptials held on July 28, 1941, at a little after one in the morning. The couple stayed at the then just opened *El Rancho Vegas* for their honeymoon.

TOP Judy and Dave in the music room of their honeymoon home.

BOTTOM The couple arrive at Union Station.

When news of the marriage reached MGM, studio executives were furious and demanded that Judy return immediately to the studio to begin her new picture, *Babes on Broadway*. Judy had no choice but to return to Hollywood.The Roses purchased the old mansion once belonging to Jean Harlow and set up houskeeping. Above, Judy and Dave in the music room of their home and, below, arriving at Union Station.

TOP Judy and Dave at the Ambassador Hotel in late 1941

BOTTOM Judy, Dave and famed Hollywood gossip columnist, Hedda Hopper.

Although happy for a short time, Judy began returning home to her mother and sisters for days at a time and Judy even asked Ethel to accompany the couple on a trip to New York for several weeks. Many have speculated as to why the Rose marriage did not work. Some have said that Dave would work nonstop on his music for hours through the night with no desire to talk or interact with anyone including his wife, then sleep for most of the day, while Judy would work during the day, then seek his company for dinner and an early evening. Others maintained that Judy and Dave were complete opposites, not only in their work routines, but also in their personalities. Judy was outgoing, fun-loving and energetic while Dave was low- key, aloof and serious. Judy was still considered a "young girl," by friends and family, while Dave was referred to as "the old man" by the Garlands. Though she never said it herself, many believe that the marriage was simply a way for Judy, at age 19, to assert her independence and that David Rose just happened to be the first gentleman with whom she had become involved. Many, including Dave's first wife, Martha Raye, warned Judy not to marry hastily, but it only pushed Judy closer and faster to the altar. It would not be long before the couple would realize that the marriage had been a mistake, but first Uncle Sam needed them both.

TOP Judy and Dave December 6, 1941.
BOTTOM The last photograph taken of Judy and Dave together in December 1942.

"I was much too young, but you couldn't have made me believe that then. Mom tried to tell me; so did everyone else."

- Judy Garland on her first marriage to David Rose

Though in place for several months previous, Mr. & Mrs. Rose formally announced their separation just after Dave left for the military. Years after Judy's death, there was speculation that an incident of illness had actually been a cover for a pregnancy terminated on the order of either Judy's mother or MGM.This report of an abortion appeared only after Judy's death in a brief, unpublished work.The statement was based upon hearsay and was never reported publicly by Judy. There was never public confirmation of either a pregnancy or an abortion occurring during Judy's marriage to David Rose and both matters remain purely speculative.

TOP Mickey, Judy and director Busby Berkeley during the filming of 1941's *Babes on Broadway*.

BOTTOM Berkeley directs Judy and Mickey in the filming of the "Hoedown" dance number.

Recognizing the dynamite team they had in Garland and Rooney, MGM carefully crafted the duo in several big musical films, all under the supervision of a director named Busby Berkeley, a man some people considered a genius, while others called a monster. Berkeley's style of directing involved numerous rehearsals and takes. Judy was always known as a one-take performer, and she grew increasingly resentful of Berkeley's constant barking of orders. Said Judy in later years of Berkeley, "I used to feel as if he had a big, black bull whip and he was lashing me with it." Despite Berkeley's foul manner, Judy enjoyed her time working in these films and Mickey's presence made the effort all the more pleasant.

Jack Paar to Judy on his 1965 television show:

"Whom did you really love at MGM?"

Judy's repsonse: "Mr. Mayer and Mickey Rooney."

Mickey & "Joots"

• Mickey Rooney was born Joseph Yule, Jr. on September 24, 1920 in Brooklyn, New York. He was the only child of Vaudeville performers who divorced when he was a toddler. He made his feature film debut in 1927, playing a cigar-smoking midget in *Orchids and Ermine*, but had appeared previously since the age of 18 months on stage with his parents.

• Rooney also starred in a series of comedies based on the "Toonerville Trolley" comic strip. He played "Mickey McGuire" in dozens of shorts from 1927 to 1934. He tried to change his name to Mickey McGuire, but had to settle for Rooney.

• Mickey was signed by MGM to a contract in 1935. Previously he had appeared in more than a dozen films including *Manhattan Melodrama*, *A Midsummer Night's Dream* and *Ah, Wilderness*. After appearing with Spencer Tracy and Freddie Bartholomew in *Captains Courageous*, Mickey played Andy Hardy in the hugely popular Hardy Family series of films.

• Mickey Rooney was crowned King of Hollywood in 1939, upsetting Shirley Temple as the number one box office draw. Rooney went on to star in numerous films including the dramas, *The Human Comedy*, *Young Tom Edison* and *National Velvet*. Several directors, including Clarence Brown, termed young Rooney the finest actor they had ever directed.

• Judy Garland and Mickey Rooney teamed for the first time in 1937's *Thoroughbreds Don't Cry*. It would be the only time that Judy would receive billing over Mickey Rooney in a picture.

• Mickey and Judy made a total of ten pictures together: *Thoroughbreds Don't Cry, Love Finds Andy Hardy, Babes in Arms, Andy Hardy Meets Debutante, Strike Up the Band, Life Begins for Andy Hardy, Babes on Broadway, Thousands Cheer, Girl Crazy,* and *Words and Music.* All together Mickey Rooney has made over 240 films.

• Mickey and Judy first met at the Lawlor Professional School for Children, a private school for child entertainers in Hollywood. Mickey was in the eighth grade and Judy, (still known then as Baby Gumm) was in the sixth grade. Mickey soon left the Lawlor school for private tutoring at MGM after he was signed to a contract.

• Mickey affectionately called Judy "Joots" because he said, "It just takes too long to get out Judy."

• Although in later years, when under the stress of emotional, physical or financial problems, Judy Garland would speak negatively of MGM's treatment of her and Mickey, Rooney has always denied this.

• In addition to their film work, Judy and Mickey would appear together on radio broadcasts and at studio functions, as well as make numerous personal appearances. While the pair was often photographed and seen together, there was never any serious speculation of romantic feelings between them, and the two always said that they thought of one another as they would a brother or sister.

"During those incredible, wonderful, vanished years, I was still growing up. So was Judy. Her life perfectly matched mine. Our friendship grew stronger and stronger." - Mickey Rooney

TOP Judy and her nearly lifelong musical director, Roger Edens and, in rear, conductor George Stoll.

BOTTOM Judy's first live concert appearance on July 9, 1943 at The Robin Hood Dell Ampitheatre in Philadelphia, PA.

Although they had actually parted by February 1942, the formal separation between Judy and David Rose was not announced until December 1942 when Dave entered the Army Air Corps. However expected it may have been, Judy was clearly saddened by the demise of her first marriage, and neither she nor David Rose ever expressed a bad word for each other. Judy now threw herself into her work including a much anticipated first live concert with an orchestra under the direction of Andre Kostelanetz. Judy also undertook several major studio projects at this time including the films *For Me and My Gal* and *Presenting Lily Mars.*

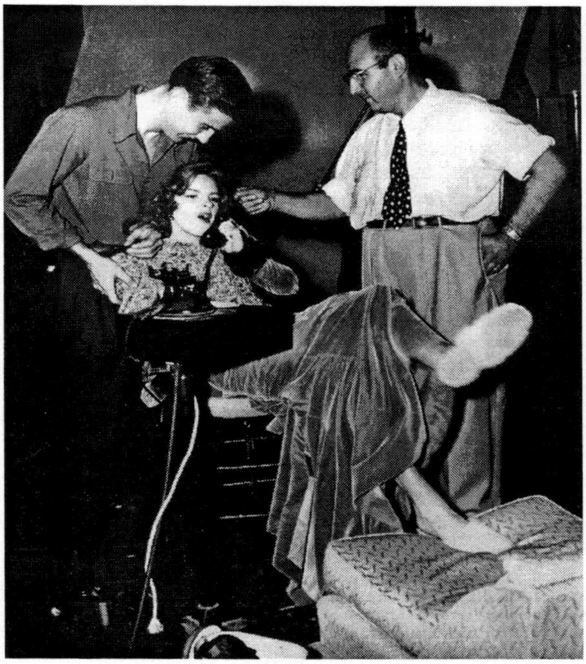

THIS PAGE Judy on the set of *Presenting Lily Mars* with co-star Van Heflin and director Joe Pasternak.

An ever increasing work load consisting of films, radio, live performances and war efforts began to take its toll on Judy. In later years, Judy would note this time period as the true beginning of her erratic sleep patterns. This necessitated her use of sleeping pills to gain rest, then amphetamines to counteract the sedatives' effects and to help maintain her figure which, due to her now adult roles, had to always be on the slender side. "Diets were not for me," she would explain, "so I stuck to the pills without really knowing their effects on me." Although Judy did manage many times when she did not need to rely on any type of medication, this pattern of pill taking would grow steadily as the years passed by.

TOP Judy is accompanied by an army band while visiting a military training center. Judy's first appearance at an army camp was in January 1942 and included her then husband David Rose, seen here at the piano. (Judy and Dave *unofficially* separated as soon as they returned to Hollywood the following month.) Although she expressed a great desire to entertain troops abroad, Judy's wartime service would be limited to the United States.

TOP Judy eagerly did whatever she could for the war effort. Here she poses with a V-bag (V for Victory, that is), promoted for use to carry home one's own purchases so as to ease gasoline and tire consumption used by delivery trucks, as well manpower needed elsewhere. Judy's V-bag declares, "I'll carry mine."

BOTTOM Judy poses with a galaxy of Hollywood stars at the Treasury Department's *Back The Attack* Show. On the stage are Dick Powell, Fred Astaire, Betty Hutton, Kay Kyser, Greer Garson, Judy, Mickey Rooney, Harpo Marx, James Cagney, Lucille Ball, and Kathryn Grayson.

"Imagine me bombing Hitler twice a day!"

- Judy Garland upon hearing that the US Army Air Corps had two bombers named after her.

During World War II Judy sought to donate as much of her time and talent to the war effort as possible. The Hollywood Canteen was a favorite spot for servicemen to enjoy the entertainment of their favorite stars free of charge. Hollywood's biggest stars all appeared at the club, a converted old barn located on Cahuenga Boulevard, to entertain or visit with the troops. Friday night was "MGM Night" at the Hollywood Canteen. Judy was one of the most popular entertainers with servicemen receiving thousands of letters and gifts from military camps around the world. During the air war with Germany, it was common for the crew of a bomber to name their carrier after a favorite female. When Judy learned that there were two United States bombers named, "The Judy Garland," she was deeply moved and exclaimed, "Imagine me bombing Hitler twice a day!"

Judy wows some servicemen in 1943.

At ease, Miss Garland!

Judy took part in several military base tours and enjoyed telling this story about her early camp tours: "I was the first of the picture people to make a camp tour and I didn't know what the insignia meant. So I called a colonel a corporal; a brigadier-general, a lieutenant and so on. At Camp Walters in Arkansas, I pulled several of these boners, which certainly got me the laughs when I least expected them. After I got home, the boys sent me a whole chart with all the insignia and what they mean. My sisters hung it in the dining room at home so that I can study it while we eat dinner. I'm living and learning, General!"

During the war, sugar was rationed and one army camp, upon learning that Judy loved chocolate candy, was so thrilled that Judy had visited with them, that they sent all their candy rations to Judy. In September 1943, Judy was asked to take part in a grand war effort known as "The Hollywood Bond Cavalcade." Hitting sixteen cities in three weeks, the tour had as its primary objective the raising of funds through the sale of war bonds. The group consisted of such luminaries as Lucille Ball, Greer Garson, Mickey Rooney, Kathryn Grayson, Fred Astaire, Jose Iturbi and Harpo Marx among others. The tour played to nearly ten million fans, each of whom had to buy a $25 war bond as admission.

TOP On radio with Meredith Wilson, Frank Morgan, and The Andrews Sisters

BOTTOM New York City July 1943 on a tour of East Coast Military camps.

"Judy is the girl every guy dreams of coming home to." - General Stephen Walters, Ft. Riley,

Judy, accompanied by her mother, completed several tours of Army camps, military hospitals and USO centers. Judy insisted on eating with the enlisted men rather than with the commanding officers until the mess hall at one camp erupted in near riot upon her arrival. On several occasions, Judy took the telephone number of a few servicemen, then gave each family a call to tell them that their son or husband was doing well. Said one army general, "Judy is the girl every guy dreams of coming home to."

TOP Judy is surrounded by music and merriment as she lets loose with a good laugh while appearing on an AFR (Armed Forces Radio) broadcast with Jimmy Durante, Bing Crosby and Meredith Wilson. Nearly everyone who truly knew Judy was sure to mention how much she enjoyed laughing - and how much more she enjoyed making others laugh right along with her!

BOTTOM Judy jokes with Harpo Marx while critically acclaimed classical pianist Jose Iturbi tries to provide a melody on the train piano. Judy worked with Jose Iturbi several times during the 1940's, both in radio and in film, most memorably in their specialty number "The Joint is Really Jumpin' Down at Carnegie Hall," which they performed to rave reviews in the film *Thousands Cheer.*

After her divorce from David Rose, Judy was often shown in photo spreads as a mature, independent and self-reliant young woman enjoying her life. Little mention of a first marriage was ever made again. David Rose, remarried with two daughters, enjoyed a successful music career well into the 1980's, which included the composition of a number one hit record ("The Stripper"), as well as several very well-known television theme songs.He passed away in 1996.

Judy is shown in publicity stills balancing the household budget and baking a cake, but the reality was that she almost always left the management of her financial affairs, as well as the baking of her cakes, to others. Generous and supportive to family and friends, Judy provided unselfishly and without hesitation for those she loved. (One example: After the husband of her close friend Betty Jane Graham was killed in action in 1942, Judy provided for her until she was able to work.) After their divorce, Judy sold the huge home she and David Rose had purchased upon their marriage and moved into a much smaller bungalow type home one block away from her mother in Westwood. At this time, Judy's sister Jimmie worked as a script girl for MGM and she and Judy would commute together back and forth to the studio. Jimmie Garland also pursued a career as a singer at this time, appearing at several Hollywood and New York City nightclubs.

TOP Judaline visits "Aunt Judy" on the set of the film *For Me and My Gal.* Judy was Judaline's godmother and namesake. Though named Judith Gale at birth, she was always known as Judaline and legally changed her name to such as an adult.

BOTTOM The Gumm Girls in 1943

Judy maintained a close relationship with her family through the 1940's. In early 1943, Judy returned home to live with her mother, sisters and niece in a new house in Westwood.

TOP Judy greets the guard at the MGM studio gate. Judy was often chauffered to work by a studio car , but sometimes opted to drive in with a friend or family member, especially when Jimmie Garland worked at MGM with her sister.

BOTTOM Judy in her original dressing room. MGM built more sophisticated, spacious dressing rooms after 1943.

TOP Judy in her updated dressing room

Judy reads a copy of *Movie Life* magazine while relaxing in her MGM dressing room. After 1943, MGM built more tasteful apartment-like dressing rooms for their major stars.

BOTTOM Judy and Frank Sinatra

Judy on numerous radio programs, both solo and with fellow entertainers. Judy appeared with Frank Sinatra in March 1944 on an Armed Forces Radio broadcast of "Command Performance." The two also appeared on a "March of Dimes" broadcast, a radio special entitled "Dick Tracy in B Flat," "The Jerome Kern Memorial Tribute" and several more "Command Performances." The two continued their friendship into the 1950's and '60's with Frank later appearing on one of Judy's television specials.

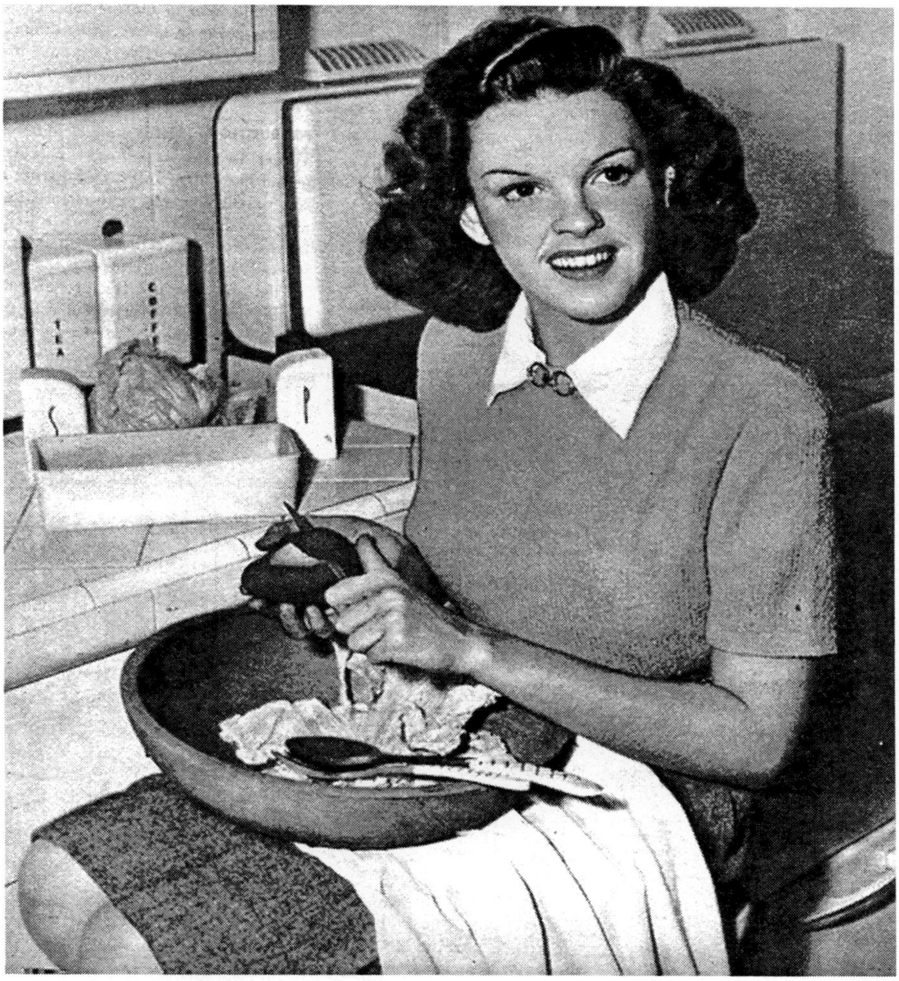

"What loused Judy up is psychiatry. She was the most happy, normal, lively, laughing girl you ever met until she began going to a psychiatrist." - Jimmie Garland

Judy may have been frequently photographed taking care of such everyday chores as preparing a salad, but the reality was that she was simply too busy to even think of such things, let alone devote any amount of time to them herself. During the period of 1942 to 1943, Judy made four feature films, *For Me and My Gal*, *Presenting Lily Mars*, *Thousands Cheer* and *Girl Crazy,* as well as numerous radio and personal appearances. In the late fall of 1943, Judy began production on her next big film, *Meet Me in St. Louis*, a work that was destined to change her very existence.

Glamour portrait circa 1943.

5

The Star

Judy Garland did not want to make *Meet Me in St. Louis*. After reviewing the initial scripts, she believed the storyline was poorly developed. In addition, the role assigned to her was that of a seventeen-year-old high school student and, after finally being accepted in adult roles, Judy was reluctant to return to playing a young girl. So unhappy was Judy with the prospect of making *Meet Me in St. Louis* that she had her mother speak with producer Arthur Freed in an effort to convince him that she was not right for the film. All of Judy's efforts, however, proved futile and she was cast in the lead role as Esther Smith in *Meet Me in St. Louis*.

Aside from the fact that *Meet Me in St. Louis* has become probably Judy's second most popular MGM film, it is also one that changed her life. Directing *Meet Me in St. Louis* was Vincente Minnelli, a much admired New York stage director brought to Hollywood by MGM. As rehearsals began for *MMISL*, Judy and Vincente were less than cordial to each other. Judy thought Vincente too critical and demanding. She said she had no idea what he wanted from her as an actress. She could not, she was sure during those early days of *MMISL*, continue to work with such a man. So she thought!

The Garland-Minnelli romance began in earnest during the last weeks of shooting on *Meet Me in St. Louis*. By 1944, Judy had matured considerably and this was evident in the way she now carried herself both in public and private. She was much more secure, self-assured and unafraid to express herself and seek out what she wanted, and Vincente certainly added to Judy's personal and public growth as both a woman and an actress.

TOP Judy, Robert Walker and Vincente enjoy some cake during a break on the set of *The Clock.*

BOTTOM Judy obliges a photographer on the set of *The Clock.* Judy reportedly went through six of these dresses in her role in the film.

During the summer of 1944 Judy filmed her part in the MGM all-star film *Ziegfeld Follies*. The film was designed to showcase MGM's stable of talent as each star took part in sketches, vignettes and musical numbers, one after the other, much like a vaudeville stage show. Although a generally poorly reviewed film, Judy's scene in *Ziegfeld Follies,* a humorous satirical piece directed by Vincente, was singled out as one of its few highlights, proving Judy's great comedic abilities.

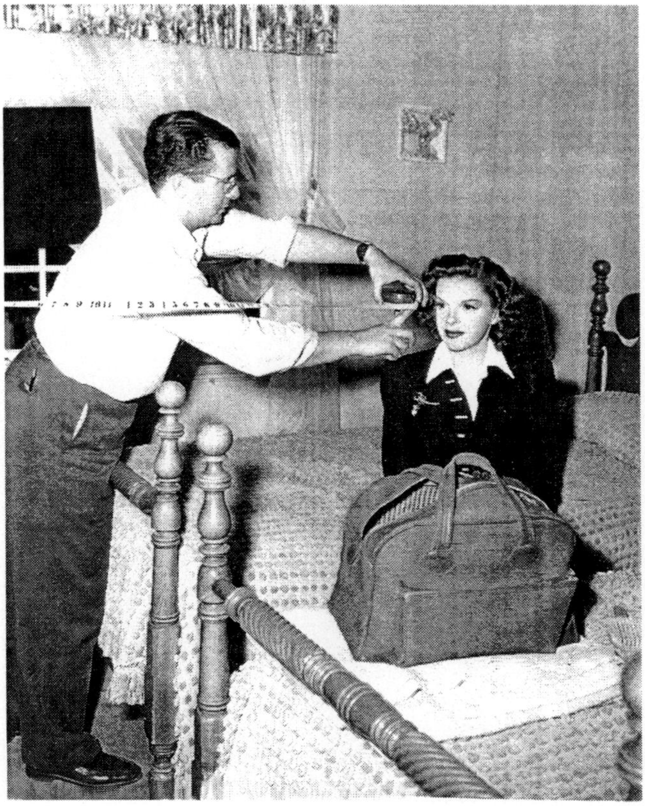

TOP and BOTTOM On the set of *The Clock*

After completing her role in *Ziegfeld Follies*, Judy reported for work on *The Clock* in October 1944. To Judy's delight, *The Clock* was a totally non-musical film. "I don't sing a note!" she happily told the press. Producer Arthur Freed said of the film, "I did *The Clock* as a kick for Judy who wanted to do a straight role. She was great, but the problem is that many people can do drama, but few can sing. The fans want to hear Judy sing." After initial director Jack Conway fell ill, Fred Zinneman was assigned to direct *The Clock*, but Judy had plans of her own in mind. Judy clearly wanted Vincente to direct *The Clock*. At Judy's request, producer Freed removed Zinneman and replaced him with Vincente, much to Judy's pleasure. Filming of *The Clock* under Vincente's direction began on November 1, 1944. The stage was now set for Judy and Vincente to produce, direct and star in their own real-life Hollywood romance.

TOP Judy and Vincente in the fall of 1944. Said Judy, "Vincente is wonderful. He's the most interesting man I've ever known. He knows everything in the world, honestly, it amazes me - he's read everything and heard every piece of music and been everywhere, but you'd never think it just to meet him, he's so quiet and rather shy and always making you laugh."

BOTTOM Judy and Vincente in the Pink and Crystal Lounge of The Ziegfeld Theatre in New York City in December 1944. The couple was photographed during intermission of *Seven Lively Arts*. Vincente had a flair for the artistic, was well read, articulate and, much to Judy's pleasure, had a wonderful sense of humor.

TOP Judy and Vincente attend the 1944 Homecoming Show at Los Angeles Memorial Coliseum.

BOTTOM Judy and Vincente relax on the 1944 set of *Ziegfeld Follies*. Vincente directed Judy's scenes in this film.

On January 9, 1945, Vincente Minnelli proposed to Judy Garland while the couple dined at The Villa Nova Restaurant (now The Rainbow Grill) on Sunset Blvd. While the morning newspapers happily proclaimed the news of Judy and Vincente's engagement, work obligations, along with the wait for Judy's divorce from David Rose to become final, would postpone the wedding ceremony for a few months.

"We were so happy. There were sad times to be sure, but they were so minor compared to what we usually had."

- Vincente Minnelli on his marriage to Judy Garland

On June 8, 1945, Judy's divorce became final and on June 11, she and Vincente applied for a marriage license. The original wedding plans called for a New York City setting and Vincente made arrangements to transport their family and a few friends to New York. The Manhattan plans were scrapped, however, when Louis B. Mayer could not make the trip and expressed great disappointment at having to miss the event, especially since he had been asked to give away the bride. The wedding took place on Friday, June 15, 1945 in the backyard of the home Judy shared with her mother and sisters.

Now Mr. and Mrs. Vincente Minnelli, the couple left the evening of their wedding on a train bound for New York City where they would spend the next ten weeks. Occupying a penthouse on Sutton Place, the city's most exclusive street, Judy and Vincente filled their days with museums, theatre, clubs, weekends trips to the Long Island shore, as well as a short trip to Boston. Prior to her relationship with Vincente, Judy had increased her use of prescription amphetamines for energy and weight control. Both Judy and Vincente knew that this was not good. It was during the Minnellis' honeymoon that Judy, feeling relaxed, hopeful, loved and secure with her new husband, would throw away her pills for a good amount of time. Vincente also recounted a humorous event during their honeymoon when Gobo, their poodle pictured above, was lost in the vast city and an all out police dragnet was cast for the pooch.

Vincente Minnelli

• Vincente Minnelli was born on February 28, 1903 in Chicago, Illinois and died July 25, 1986 in Beverly Hills, California.

• Vincente was born Lester Anthony Minnelli to Vincente and Mina Minnelli. He was their only child to survive to adulthood, having lost two previous sons in infancy. Minnelli took his father's name as a young man.

• Vincente came from a theatre family, The Minnelli Brothers Tent Show Theatre.

• Vincente first worked as a costume designer for a Chicago theatre, then made his way to Broadway where worked as a set designer. He was hired as the art director for the famed Radio City Musical Hall in 1935.

• Vincente Minnelli designed the famous wooden soldier costumes still used today by the Radio City Rockettes. He was the scenic designer for *Earl Carroll's Vanities* in 1935.

• Vincente also worked as a director, with his first directorial project being *At Home Abroad*. Vincente then moved on to work with the *Ziegfled Follies of 1936*.

• Minnelli authored his first book show, *The Show is On,* which was produced in 1937 and starred Beatrice Lillie and Bert Lahr.

• After Broadway's *Hooray for What!* and *Very Warm for May*, Minnelli was brought out to Hollywood by Arthur Freed to work for MGM in 1940. Vincente started out at MGM as a jack-of-all-trades before making his directorial debut with *Cabin in the Sky*.

• Vincente worked in an uncredited background capacity on two of Judy Garland's early films, *Babes on Broadway* and *Strike Up the Band*. (Minnelli devised the animated fruit sequence in the latter.)

• Though he directed all kinds of films, Vincente Minnelli is best remembered as the father of the innovative, creative and lavish movie musical. Many of Minnelli's films featured elaborate dream or dance sequences filled with huge sets, lavish costumes and rich, sumptuous colors.

• It has been said that it didn't matter what kind of film Vincente Minnelli undertook; they all had taste and style. Vincente was devoted to MGM, working countless hours to develop some of the most beloved and famous films ever made.

• Vincente Minnelli received the Academy Award for Best Director for 1958's *Gigi*.

• Vincente Minnelli was married a total of four times, in order, Judy Garland, Georgette Magnani, Diana Hale, and his last wife, Lee Anderson Minnelli, who has been his widow since 1986.

• Vincente Minnelli is the father of Liza Minnelli and Christina Minnelli and the grandfather of two.

• After his death, an anonymous source spoke of Minnelli as being a closet homosexual, however, the facts indicate that no man has ever claimed to have shared such a relationship with Vincente, that Vincente never lived with any man in Chicago, New York City or Hollywood, that none of his wives ever made a claim as such, that no one has ever gone on record with such a claim and that a story placing Vincente in such a relationship has its foundation in a singular, anonymous source.

TOP Judy and Vincente with Hedda Hopper at The Stork Club in New York City. While in New York, Judy and Vincente hosted a party for Vincente's theatre friends. After the guests had all departed, Vincente, completely seduced by Judy's poise, charm and manner, declared to his new wife, "I think I'll keep you."

BOTTOM Completely oblivious to the photographer, Judy is absorbed in her husband. Some have claimed that the Minnelli-Garland union was an escape for the latter and a cover for the former. No one has ever claimed to have shared such a relationship with Vincente, and a story placing him in such a position has its foundation in a singular, anonymous source. Said the four times married (and father of two) Vincente himself, "We were so happy. There were sad times to be sure, but they were so minor compared to what we usually had." Said Judy of her husband, "Vincente is my greatest love-and my best friend."

TOP Judy and Vincente relax in their home which featured hundreds of books, recordings, antiques, and artwork. After their marriage, the couple moved into Vincente's bachelor house which they promptly had remodeled to a larger size. So extensive were the renovations, that the couple was forced to relocate for a short time to a rented home in Malibu.

BOTTOM Judy and Vincente at the Hollywood Bowl in 1946. An interesting note: No one could ever accuse Judy Garland of being a spendthrift on clothing. Here Judy is wearing the same fur jacket she wore at age seventeen to her hand and footprinting at Grauman's Theatre in October 1939 and again to the 1940 Academy Awards ceremony!

TOP Judy and Vincente attend a party at which George Jessel M.C.'s in costume.

MIDDLE Judy, Vincente and their studio boss, Louis. B Mayer.

Judy held L.B. Mayer in high esteem and spoke lovingly of him throughout her life, never blaming him for anything unfortunate that may have befallen her. Mayer, for his part, always held great respect and affection for the girl who had been called his all-around favorite star at the studio.

BOTTOM Judy visits with her husband on one of his sets.

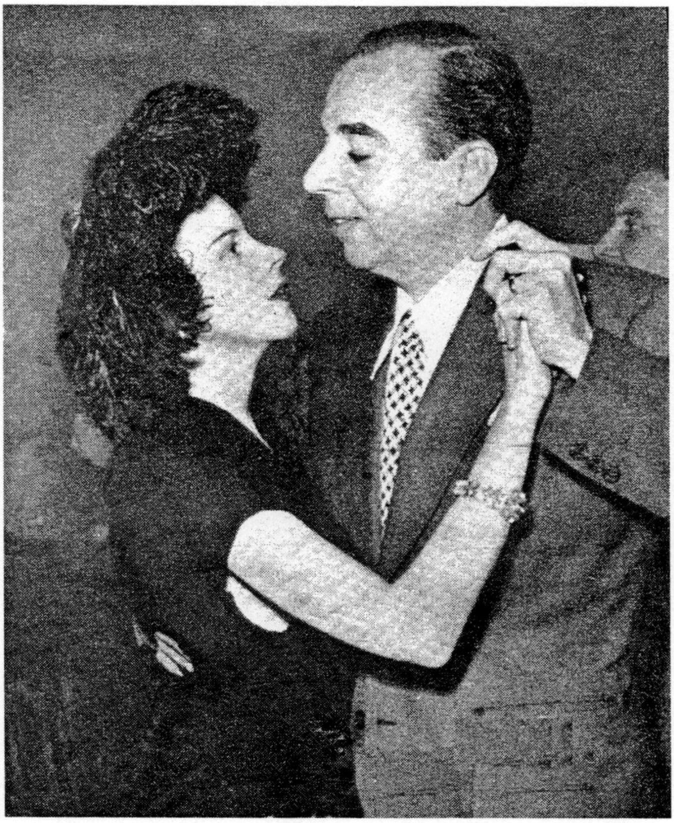

There is no doubt that the Minnellis shared a deep love, passion and affection for each other. In describing when she and Vincente disagreed on something, Judy told reporter Adela Rogers St. John, "And then do you know, how we laugh - then kiss and kiss and kiss....." while Vincente related how Judy would charm and entice him into staying home with her on a workday or on some occasion when they were expected elsewhere. Said Judy to reporter Helen Weller in 1948, "I was so touched when Vincente insisted that our wedding be a double-ring ceremony. And, do you know, that he hasn't taken it off once yet! Do you have any idea how wonderful that makes me feel?"

TOP Always popular with magazine and newspaper readers and appearing on hundreds of magazines covers, Judy sits for an interview.

BOTTOM Judy and producer Arthur Freed. Said Freed, "I regard Judy as one of the most talented and exciting people that I have ever worked with. Her drive and sincerity were a tremendous help to everyone with whom she worked. Judy gave great affection to everyone. She was always extremely cooperative with producers, directors and her fellow artists."

TOP Judy reviews some music and lyrics before recording a radio promo.

BOTTOM Though never the least pretentious, Judy possessed her own distinctive air of elegance.

In November 1946, MGM offered Judy a new seven-year contract, one which boasted a raise in salary to over $5,000 per week. Although a fantastic offer, Judy had not wanted to renew her film contract preferring to work in radio, do recordings and, hopefully, return to the live stage where she had first started. Seven more years of the hectic, stressful pace associated with movie musicals was not exactly appealing, yet she could not turn down such a lucrative offer, especially since both she and Vincente were as adept at spending money as making it, and so she began work on several new films.

TOP and BOTTOM Judy with her *Harvey Girls* co-star, John Hodiak, and filming the opening train scene.

According to some, *The Harvey Girls* was the first picture during which Judy demonstrated difficult behavior. Some say that she was irritable, unproductive and nervous while filming. Yet many others, among them co-star Ray Bolger, insist that this was completely untrue. "I worked with Judy on *The Harvey Girls*," he told a reporter years later, "and I never saw any evidence of any temperament. She was never any problem. She was always professional and considerate throughout the shoot."

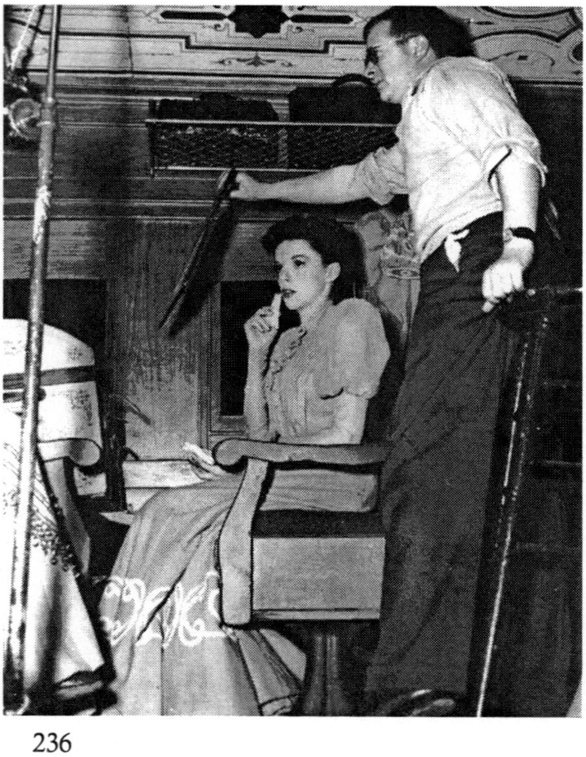

TOP Judy on the set of *Till the Clouds Roll By*.

It was Judy's performance as Marilyn Miller in *Till The Clouds Roll By*, the poorly reviewed musical bio of songwriter Jerome Kern, that claimed the movie's only good notes. Said one reviewer that, "Judy plays the part astonishingly well... it is difficult to think of anyone who could have done so more successfully."

BOTTOM Judy waves a warm hello and gives a smile while waiting to film a scene on the set of *The Harvey Girls.*

TOP Judy relaxes on her husband's lap during a break in the filming of *The Pirate*. It was during this production that Judy first experienced real difficulty in maintaining her high standard of performance.She was often late and apprehenisve about her ability to perform at her best. Director/husband Vincente provided tremendous support during this trying time as did co-stars and studio workers and there were also many light-hearted moments when Judy's laughter would fill the set.

BOTTOM Dot Ponedel, Judy's friend and personal make-up artist, applies a touch-up during *The Pirate* while everyone enjoys a light moment.

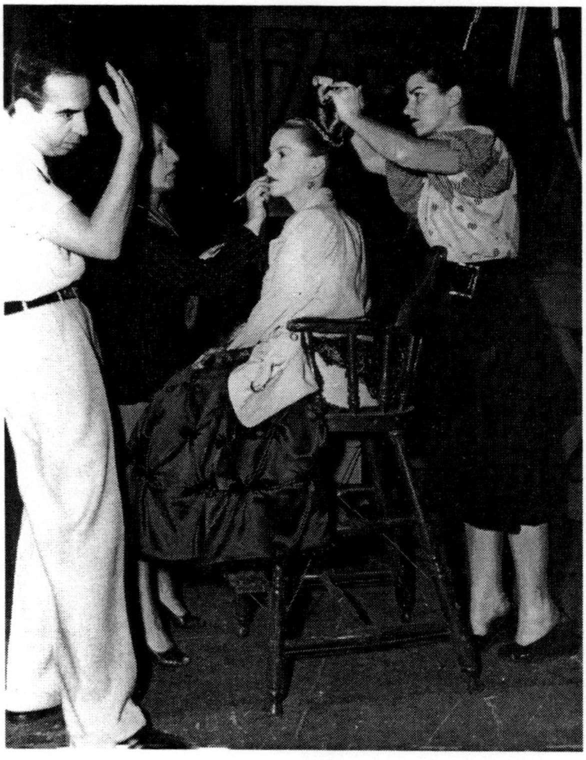

THIS PAGE Judy and Vincente on the set of *The Pirate* in 1947.

Filming on *The Pirate*, which co-starred the Minnellis' good friend, Gene Kelly, began in early February 1947 and was often delayed due to Judy's growing anxiety at this time. As anyone who ever worked with her would tell, Judy only worked when she felt she was at her best and she was now suffering a bout of true anxiety. She quickly lost confidence in herself and her abilities. Vincente, as both director and husband, exercised a tremendous amount of patience, compassion and understanding to get his wife through the film. Said Judy of this time period, "I was a nervous wreck, jumpy and irritable. I couldn't take the tension at the studio. Everything at MGM was competitive. In the movies, beauty was the standard of judgement, and this I definitely did not have. Most people can work off extra pounds, but not me. They seemed to stick to me. I found the only way I could keep my weight off - and the only way I could go to sleep - was to take pills." Judy knew she needed to rest and once filming was complete on *The Pirate*, she left for a short stay at a health facility in California, then at another in Boston, Massachusetts.

"Judy was always so cooperative. She never went 'glamour girl' on you."

- Director Chuck Walters

TOP Judy on the set of 1948's *Easter Parade*. BOTTOM Judy and Peter Lawford during a break in *Easter Parade*. In the film they performed "Fella With an Umbrella" together.

After just a few weeks, Judy felt renewed and was eager to return to Hollywood. Unfortunately, Hollywood was all too eager to get her back. No sooner was she back home than was she put to work. First, *The Pirate* had to be redone with many new scenes and retakes that ran to more than two months worth of work. In addition, filming was set to begin on *Easter Parade* co-starring Fred Astaire and directed, once again, by husband Vincente.

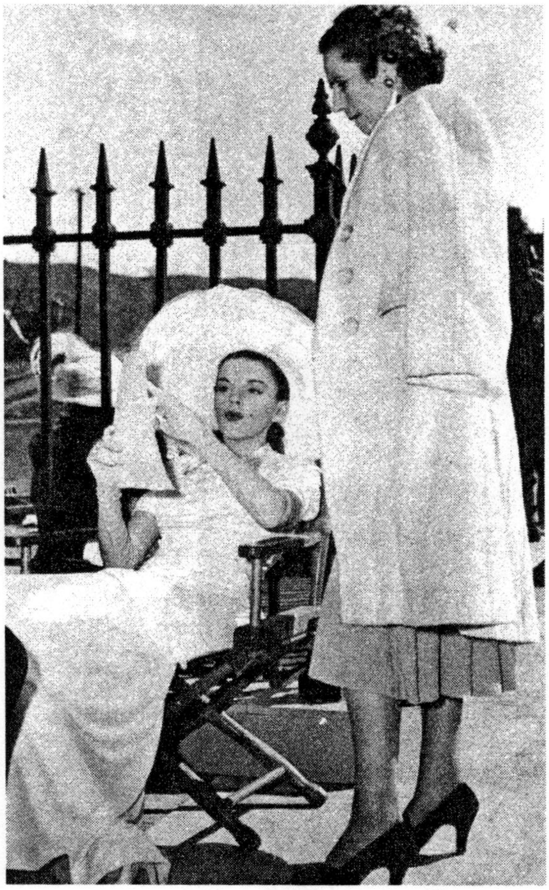

TOP Judy relaxes on the set with Fred Astaire and Chuck Walters.

BOTTOM Judy with secretary Toni DiPaola.

Tension in the Minnelli marriage was beginning to become evident during early 1948. Judy was advised by her doctor that she and Vincente should not be working so closely together on a film, then go home and try to be husband and wife. Judy and Vincente both wanted to do whatever they could to keep their marriage happy, so Vincente was replaced as director of *Easter Parade* with Chuck Walters who said of Judy, "I never had any problems with Judy. She was always cooperative. She never went 'glamour girl' on you."

"Judy's drive and sincerity were a tremendous help to everyone with whom she worked. She gave great affection to everyone."

- MGM Prodcuer Arthur Freed

TOP Costume designer Irene and producer Arthur Freed watch as Judy runs through a dance routine for *Easter Parade*. These fashion run-through's were necessary so that the designer could determine what freedom a costume must have.

BOTTOM Judy guest stars on "Perry Como's Chesterfield Supper Club" on NBC radio in May 1948.

Though Judy was always remembered for her intelligence, wit and professionalism, she did face several daunting challenges, always with much resolve and courage. Judy had been seeking therapy on and off for several years, sometimes seriously, but mostly without much intensity or focus. Soon after her separation from David Rose in 1942, Judy took up psychoanalysis, encouraged by a man upon whom she had a tremendous crush. Said sister Jimmie, "What loused Judy up is psychiatry. She was the most happy, normal, lively, laughing girl you ever met until she began going to a psychiatrist. Judy was very much in love at the time with a writer/director. The writer/director told her she was a pathological liar and should see a psychiatrist. Judy was so in love with this man, his every word was her command. Judy would go to these doctors, tell them a lot of phony, made up stories, then they would convince her that everyone was against her - her family, her friends, her studio, everyone." Judy would later agree with her sister's assessment. "I took a series of psychoanalytical treatments, and I have never regretted anything more. I'm sure that psychoanalysis has helped many people, but for me it was like taking strong medicine for a disease I didn't have."

"Judy was just great on the set and everyone involved with the film treated her with kindness, accommodation, understanding and respect."

- Van Johnson on working with Judy

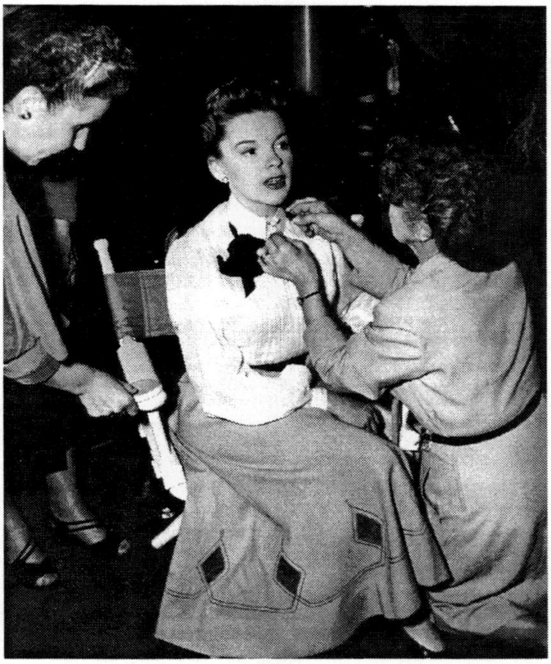

LEFT Judy clowns with fans seeking her autograph at a premiere

TOP and BOTTOM Judy on the set of *In the Good Old Summertime.*

Due to the enormous success of *Easter Parade*, MGM quickly teamed Judy and Fred again, this time in *The Barkleys of Broadway*. Unfortunately, Judy was simply too exhausted from the grueling schedule of shooting *Easter Parade* and reshooting *The Pirate* and after only three weeks of work on *Barkleys*, she simply walked away from the film. MGM had no other recourse but to suspend her. During the suspension Judy was asked (and paid) to contribute two musical numbers to the film *Words and Music*, one of which was a duet with pal Mickey Rooney that would mark the last time the two would perform together in a feature film. Although Judy was receiving medical attention, no evidence of poor health is visible in her dynamite performance. Thoroughly charming, *In the Good Old Summertime* has always been unfairly considered one of Judy's lesser films. Judy was on solid, happy ground while making this film. She had returned from a successful rest, was enjoying her marriage to Vincente and experienced no problems at all with the shoot. She turned in a first rate performance opposite Van Johnson. According to Johnson, Judy's positive experience with *Summertime* was due simply to the fact that "everyone involved with the film treated her with kindness, accommodation, understanding and respect."

Mama Ethel strikes back

Publicity about Judy began to take on a somewhat negative air during this time. Amidst reports of her increasingly unstable emotional state and suspension from MGM, magazines began running stories like "The Brutal Truth About Judy Garland" and "Judy's Darkening Rainbow." It was Ethel who immediately counteracted the unflattering reports about her daughter and her family with a lengthy article of her own appearing in magazines in mid-1949. Some excerpts included:

"I've read so much dreamed up drivel about my daughter that the time has come to set things straight," wrote Mother Gumm. "I've read that she knew little of normal youth. If Judy's youth wasn't normal, Mr. Webster had better write himself a new dictionary. No circuses, they say? She went to every circus in town and sat right down front! No children coming over? The place was full of them! No penny candy? Well, there they've got me. Judy didn't have penny candy. It was nickel candy.

"...I've read fables that sounded as though my husband and I had stuck all three children under a railroad car and ridden the rods. Poor little Judy, I've read, yanked from town to town in the middle of the night through drifts of snow. That's absolutely absurd-would Judy have been yanked anywhere in the middle of the night? She slept in her own bed, except for when crawled into mine. I've read that poor Judy led the tough life of a vaudeville kid. The weeks she played vaudeville you could count on one hand!

"...Once in a while, on weekends, all three girls would do a show at the Biltmore in Los Angeles put on by the Meglin School where they went once a week for dancing lessons. Or, when school was out, they'd play the Pike Theater in Long Beach for a couple of days. Because they wanted to, because they thought it was fun. Nobody made them. If Judy was unhappy or felt abused, I never knew it, and I would have known it, because there was precious little she didn't tell me.

"...The truth about my family is that none of us rose from the depths, and that Judy's young life was as simple and normal as the kid's next door. My daughters never missed school. They went to church and to Sunday School and they sang in the choir and they made First Communion.

"....My husband and I were always in perfect accord concerning our daughters. Being human parents, of course we were proud of Judy's voice, but we never pushed for a career. She was a child, remember."

".... I've read that their ambitious stage mother persisted in making celebrities of her daughters. That floored me. When Susie and Jimmie wanted to stop singing and get married, they stopped. Judy didn't want to stop. 'Mama,' Judy would say to me, 'If I can be a success as a singer and actress, that's all I'll ever ask of life.' I encouraged her, of course. 'If that's what you want, we'll work for it.' But I'd have encouraged her in anything she wanted to do. I don't set myself up as any model mother. I don't hold with the saying that mother knows best, I've been wrong too often. But there's one attitude I've stuck to all my days: don't force your children to anything. Whatever you force them to isn't worth a dime.

"...And this I can tell you. Suppose I'd said to Judy, 'No, I don't want you to sing, I don't want you to go into films' - she'd still be exactly where she is today. No matter what the barriers, there's a will in Judy that would have conquered them. Not the will, may I add, for money and fame. But that of the born entertainer to express herself.

"...Another thing I would like to make clear. Judy over-dieted during adolescence, they say, injuring her health. Judy never dieted during adolescence. Doesn't anyone remember her early pictures? Did she ever look frail as a young girl?"

"I've read so much dreamed up drivel about my daughter that the time has come to set things straight." - Ethel Gumm

"I took a series of psychoanalytical treatments, and I have never regretted anything more. I'm sure that psychoanalysis has helped many people, but for me it was like taking strong medicine for a disease I didn't have."

- Judy Garland

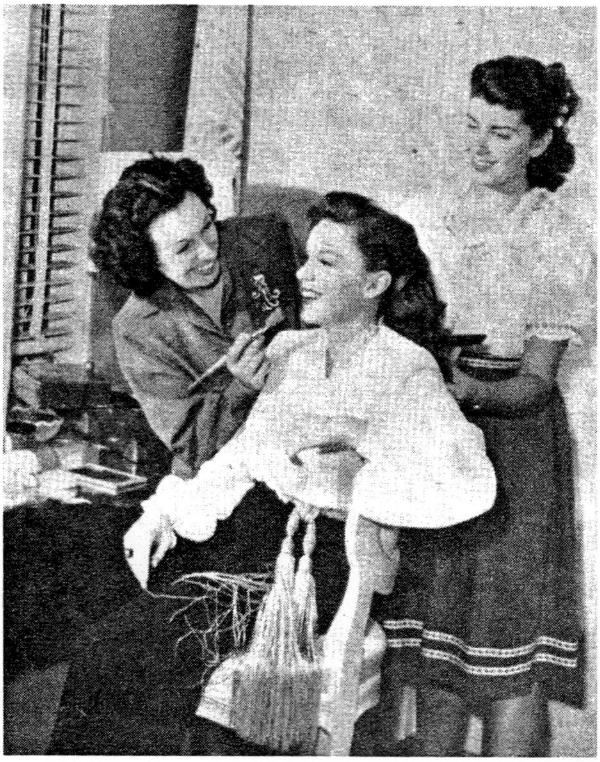

TOP Judy reviews a script in her dressing room.

BOTTOM Long time make-up director and pal, Dot Ponedel, handled Judy's make-up from 1944 onward, while Helen Young (r.) was often in charge of her hair.

ABOVE Judy and Peter Lawford at a party.

After the success of *In the Good Old Summertime*, MGM cast Judy in the film version of *Annie Get Your Gun*. Though she was initially enthusiastic about doing *Annie*, Judy was also experiencing great stress at this time, having reached the height of physical exhaustion. Due to production setbacks, Judy was forced to rehearse and/or film several lavish and involved production numbers, one after the other. Director Busby Berkeley, with whom Judy did not care to work, also added to the stress on the set. Although Berkeley was eventually replaced with pal Chuck Walters, Judy just couldn't complete the film and was replaced with Betty Hutton.

"If you really want to know who was a funny lady, it was Judy Garland. Now she was funny. I had funny writers, but Judy was naturally witty."

- Lucille Ball

Because Judy had resigned from *Annie Get Your Gun*, MGM officially placed their golden girl on suspension saying, "There is no thought of Judy's immediate reinstatement and right now there is nothing in mind regarding Miss Garland for the future." Offered Judy in response, "I don't blame the studio for suspending me. I've been a bad girl for not getting to work on time. Studios are run to make money. They can't take chances with careless people like me. I'm going to forget about work for the next year. I think I'll travel and see how the rest of the world lives. This isn't the end of me. I'm young and have years of acting and singing ahead of me."

TOP and BOTTOM The Minnellis with Carlton Alsop and his wife, Sylvia Sidney. Alsop served as Judy's manager during the later 1940's.

At the end of May 1949, Judy left Hollywood and registered at Peter Bent Brigham Hospital in Boston, Massachusetts where she concentrated on nothing more than resting, relaxing and eating well. Said Judy of her Boston stay, "The best thing about that whole stay was patching it up with Vincente. I realized that he wanted *me*, not some hypothetical creature." Vincente joined Judy in Boston, then the couple returned to Hollywood with a renewed love for each other and a strong hope of staying together.

TOP Judy and Vincente visit with Judy's sister after Jimmie's opening at Slapsie Maxie's in 1949. With them are Jimmie's second husband, Johnny Thompson, and her then eleven-year-old daughter, Judaline.

BOTTOM Judy with Esther Williams, star of numerous MGM water-based film extravaganzas.

By August 1949, it was thought that Judy was ready to return to filmmaking. *Summer Stock* went into production, but Judy soon found that she had returned to full time work too soon after her much needed rest.

THIS PAGE Judy and Vincente circa 1949.

Early on during the production of *Summer Stock*, Judy could sense that she still was not ready to return to films full-time and personally asked Louis B. Mayer for release from her contract then and there. L.B.Mayer, however, had other ideas and put all of his energy into convincing Judy to stay on, so back she went to the set.

TOP Judy and Vincente at the theatre

BOTTOM Judy and Vincente at a Don Loper Fashion Show

Judy performed well in *Summer Stock* even though her changeable emotional and physical states, along with the usual productions setbacks and delays for which she bore no responsibility, did cause a few problems on the set. "We got through *Summer Stock*, but not without a struggle," said Judy. "Gene (Kelly who co-starred) encouraged me to forget what people might be saying, laughed with me, helped keep the friction down." Judy completed *Summer Stock* by March and then left for a vacation in Carmel, California. It was decided that some scenes in *Summer Stock* had to be added and Judy was called back from her vacation. The scenes added included the famous "Get Happy" number that soon became one of Judy's most famous routines. Judy returned to her vacation, but when MGM suddenly assigned her another role in *Royal Wedding* with Fred Astaire, she found herself back before the cameras. But, again, it was too soon. *Royal Wedding* started out well, but after a few weeks, Judy just could not keep herself going and began to miss rehearsals. MGM suspended her once again and Judy was now both physically and emotionally exhausted. Feeling humiliated and unloved, taken totally by surprise at being released from *Royal Wedding* and suspended, Judy locked herself in the bathroom of the Minnelli home and, using a piece of glass from a broken tumbler, made a tiny scrape across her neck.

TOP Waiting on the *Summer Stock* set.
BOTTOM Judy with *Stock* director Chuck Walters.

According to all press reports, the self-inflicted cut was little more than a scratch. Judy's physician reported that he had examined her thoroughly and concluded that the cut required no medical attention. Several years earlier Judy had taken a similar action, scratching her wrist in the same fashion. After Vincente and Ethel calmed her down, Ethel simply covered the scratch with a small adhesive bandage. The event was never reported. This all would have also remained undisclosed to the public except for the careless remarks of a household employee who leaked the story to the press. The entire course of events was little more than a cry for attention but, unfortunately, all of the attention came from the media who was soon setting up camp near the Minnelli home. Reports of all sorts filled the newspapers and the reaction was one of sympathy for Judy. Fans around the world loved her all the more and eagerly sent her their support.

TOP Judy and Eddie Bracken on the *Summer Stock* set. BOTTOM Judy gets a touch up on the set

Over the years, the story has been concocted (recently reinforced with the aid of television) that Ethel had been turned away from seeing Judy at the time. This is completely false. Ethel was one of the first people summoned to Judy's side and one of only a few permitted access to her. As always, Ethel provided complete support of Judy as she acted as the family spokesperson, providing information to reporters: "....Of course Judy was upset. For the first few minutes all I did was hold my little girl, and then we talked. She told me that she was, 'upset and hysterical and disappointed' over losing a part. I told her that everyone feels like doing that at sometime or other. She told me that she was 'embarrassed and surprised' by the worldwide attention her actions brought. 'Isn't it awful, Mama?' she said. "....Now she's read all the wonderful telegrams and letters she's received from people all over the world. She told me, 'I didn't know I had so many friends!'

"....Judy is back to her old vital self already. Vincente is wonderful and has provided Judy with such gentle care and support.

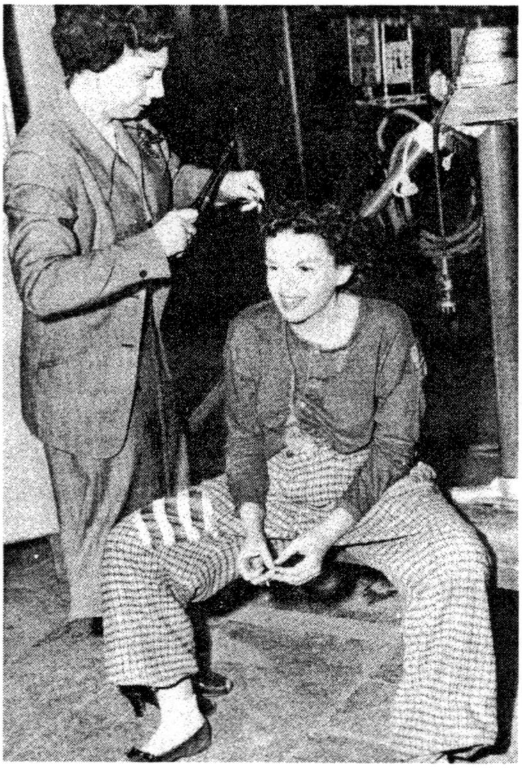

"....Judy is now sleeping beautifully without having to take any sedatives. She used to take sleeping pills. When you have to get all worked up for scenes in a movie it's hard to come home, relax and sleep easily.

"...Judy is swimming, reading, resting and eating. She feels better, but we want her to stay that way. She's beginning to appreciate all the wonderful things she has, but I told her that it doesn't mean a thing if she doesn't have her health. She originally got sick a couple of years ago because she worked too hard without any break. I would like her take a year off." Several weeks later, a newspaper printed an interview with an unidentified "friend" (later said to be Sylvia Sidney) who publicly offered to "take Judy into my home and give her the tender care and loving environment that she missed in childhood." Ethel Gumm lost no time in responding. Enlisting the aid of several Hollywood reporters who knew first hand the life Judy had experienced in the Garland home, Ethel countered with her own public statement that, "Judy has always had the best care and a very loving environment throughout her life, including in childhood." While the matter disappeared quickly, little did Ethel know that her self-defense against rumors and gossip concerning her and her family had only just begun. (TOP Cary Grant visits the set of Summer Stock.)

"It wasn't a good experience, but I think I'm better for it. You're always better for the tough things if you can get through them. The tension broke and I had time for reflection." - Judy Garland commenting on her emotional distress

About those tapes.....

Judy leads a sing-a-long with Irving Berlin and Louis B. Mayer c.1948.

Over the past thirty plus years, many claims have been made regarding Judy Garland. Some have reflected the contents of audiotapes Judy made, while others have referred to the beginning notes to an autobiography from the early 1960's. Both of these sources have been liberally quoted in previous Garland projects dating back to the 1960's and although seemingly in Judy's own words, these works are not at all completely or accurately reflective of her life.

In 1959, Judy accepted an offer from world-renowned Random House book chief, Bennett Cerf, to write her autobiography. Judy did indeed start to record a small amount of commentary for the possibility of inclusion (after review and editing which she never did) in an autobiography. Judy's recorded comments are devoted to warm and loving memories of her childhood, her family, her children.

The idea for an autobiography was abandoned rather quickly, however, and it must be noted that the brief autobiographical manuscript was actually done later by at least one known ghostwriter and editor, that more than sixty-eight pages would never be completed, were never reviewed by Judy and were *previously presented* in edited forms and without her input.

Bennett Cerf went on to sell what he had of Judy's musings, (he had paid for them with an advance from the publishing house) to *McCall's* magazine, which published the work in a two-part article entitled, "There'll Always be an Encore."

There are several other tape recordings, made over the course of several years during the 1960's, that, together with Judy's first recordings, have circulated for more than three decades. Most of these later recordings, undertaken at physically, emotionally and financially stressful periods in Judy's life, were made to meet her own personal needs at that time and were never intended for public consumption.

During a particularly difficult time in her life, a friend had suggested that Judy record her thoughts as a way of dealing with the stress she was feeling. Judy herself says in the tapes that she was "going through so many moods" and that everything on the tapes will "have to be straightened out." Judy, alone in a London Hotel, venting her anger over her battle for her children, her relationship with the likes of Mark Herron, manager, David Begelman, etc. were clearly not attempts to write a book. Predictably, it has been only those isolated and distorted expressions of inner and outer conflict that have ever been made public, and without any regard or provision for at least a little perspective.

All of these tape recordings remained in the possession of either Judy or her family until, it has been said, they were taken by an employee who made copies of the tapes and circulated them among fans. (These tapes remain available today.) Some have said that the tapes show Judy inebriated or under medication, however many of the tapes were re-recorded under doctored means, purposely slowing or manipulating the recording mechanism in order to obtain the desired effect.

Others have said that Judy dictated notes concerning intimate acts, private affairs, a supposed abortion, however this is false. Reports of these and other matters appeared only *after* Judy's death and were based solely on hearsay provided by a writer, and not from Judy herself.

Judy Garland Gives Her All When She Belts Out A Song

She Loves To Perform

WHEN Judy Garland made her night club debut in Las Vegas last month a plane load of Hollywood press flew up for the event. Most of them have known Judy Garland since she was a kid star. They have reported all of her emotional binges. They have been excluded from her sets when she was working. They are bored with the Garland legend. Their attitude plainly was "Show me you're good. Prove it."

Most of them were going to Las Vegas for the ride. Some hoped that Judy would pull a Mario Lanza and refuse to show up at the last moment. As always the Garland formula of corn plus talent worked. Judy won her audience and superlatives were the order of the day.

No one has been able to define what it is that makes Judy Garland unique. Two producers at M-G-M, Arthur Freed, who helped discover her, and Joe Pasternak, who made many of her pictures, say it's a combination of emotion and hysterical talent.

It's impossible to watch Judy rehearse or work without participating. She gives everything she has, even in rehearsal. When she performs she bursts the seams of her ability. Unlike Bing Crosby or Frank Sinatra

Most of them were going to Las Vegas for the ride. Some hoped that Judy would pull a Mario Lanza and refuse to show up at the last moment. As always the Garland formula of corn plus talent worked. Judy won her audience and superlatives were the order of the day.

No one has been able to define what it is that makes Judy Garland unique. Two producers at M-G-M, Arthur Freed, who helped discover her, and Joe Pasternak, who made many of her pictures, say it's a combination of emotion and hysterical talent.

It's impossible to watch Judy rehearse or work without participating. She gives everything she has, even in rehearsal. When she performs she bursts the seams of her ability. Unlike

form, Judy is a dynamo of energy. She has a compulsion to make people listen.

A Born Performer, She Loves To Sing

"I love to sing—it's the most wonderful feeling there is in the world for me," says Judy. She proves it every time she goes out to perform. As a result, her entire career has been plagued with periods of complete physical exhaustion.

After each of her two-a-night performances in Las Vegas Judy returned to her dressing room, shut the door and slept. Her entire life was keyed to one thing—the performance.

Even at Hollywood parties Judy is an entertainer. Let some one tinkle a tune on a piano, and if she knows a lyric

JUDY GARLAND
On stage, she's dynamo of energy

Entire Life Keyed To It

she will begin to whisper i softly, then close her eyes throw her head back and sing

It's not that she's a ha[r] She's just a born performer.

Judy is a perfectionist. At r[e]cording or filming sessions she doesn't like what she hea[rs] or does she will insist on r[e]doing it over and over until sh[e] is satisfied. This desire for pe[r]fection ran up the budget [of] "A Star Is Born" from $2,500,000 to $4,500,000, but when th[e] film was completed Judy wa[s] satisfied that it was as perfe[ct] as she could make it.

Fans Insist That Judy Keep Act The Same

There are people who sa[y] that when you've seen Jud[y] Garland once you've seen he[r] for all time. Her fans insi[st] that nothing about their id[ol] change. Part of this is based o[n] the curious identification man[y] people have with Judy. Thank[s] to the wide publicity she ha[s] been given, they have lived he[r] life right along with her, an[d] as long as she stays young—and the same—so do they.

It was certain when Jud[y] opened at the Palace last wee[k] that she would wear her ol[d] tramp costume at least onc[e] during the performance; she'[d] appear in a short skirted out[fit] designed to show off th[e] maximum length of leg at leas[t] once; and that she would clos[e] her act singing "Over the Rain[bow]" with a throb in her voic[e] and a tear in her eye. And tha[t] at some time during the ac[t] her voice would break in tha[t] funny way, and she'd addres[s] the audience informally, prob[ably] to ask them if they min[d] if she lights a cigarette.

These are the standard ingredients of every Judy Garland performance whether on TV, on stage or in a night club. People have come to expect them of Judy. Although she would like to give them something different, she's typed. She's doomed, like Sophie Tucker, who has had to go down through the ages singing "Some of These Days."

There are reasons, however, for her routines. For example,

Judy always shows her legs, not so much because they are

Newspapers gave Judy's July 16, 1956 Las Vegas debut full page coverage.

6

The Artist

It wasn't long after her difficulties of June 1950 that Judy began to feel like her old self again. Encouraged by family and friends, she left for a short holiday in New York City. While there, Judy spoke with columnist Earl Wilson, telling him that she had found "new hope," called the recent past events "kid's stuff," and declared that "that's all in the past now." Judy expressed a desire for a year-long rest and, at the time, was planning on a vacation with her husband in Europe where Vincente would be working on a film. Judy credited Vincente greatly for keeping her spirit alive. "Vincente convinced me to come to New York and had some friends take me to the Capitol where my film *Summer Stock* is playing. The crowd was wonderful. They made me feel wonderful. Vincente said that that would happen. My husband always knows just what to say and do, it seems. Of course, he was right about everything."

Upon her return to Hollywood in September, Judy advised MGM executives for a second time that she wanted to be released from her contract. No one at MGM pressured her to alter her decision this time, as studio executives were reluctant to keep Judy on believing that she had lost her box-office draw and would not bring in the dollars.The story has been passed along that Judy was fired from MGM, but that is untrue. Judy knew she needed a rest and a change, something away from the filmmaking that, although it had been her lifeblood for fifteen years, had become her greatest torture. Louis B. Mayer did not, in fact, want to let Judy go. It had always been said that Judy had been Mr. Mayer's favorite child star, if not all around favorite star, on the studio lot and he expressed genuine regret at losing her. His suggestion to keep Judy on board while continuing to help her was overruled by the new executive staff and on September 29, 1950, Judy Garland and Metro-Goldwyn-Mayer Studios parted company. It may have been by mutual consent, but Louis B. Mayer was still disappointed. "She had to go," he said. "It broke my heart."

"It is with great reluctance that Judy's request has been granted, and we wish her all the success and happiness in the continuance of her career."

- MGM Studios

TOP While in New York City in August/September 1950, Judy appeared on "The Jack Eigen Morning Show." Callers filled the switchboard with expressions of love and support.

BOTTOM November 5 1950.

Judy appearing in "Alice Adams" on NBC's "The Theatre Guild on the Air." Judy loved appearing on radio shows declaring, "Radio is for me." Unfortunately, she found her favorite broadcast medium just as it began its decline in favor of that burgeoning new medium called television.

"They were terribly nice about letting me out of my contract - it was fine of them and good for me."

-Judy Garland

TOP December 1950.

Mr. and Mrs. Vincente Minnelli attend a party, the last event at which they would photographed together.

BOTTOM March 22, 1951.

Judy leaves L.A. courthouse on the arm of her lawyer after filing divorce papers for the dissolution of her marriage to Vincente Minnelli. Judy never had a bad word to say against her second husband, expressed a deep love for him, sought his advice regularly over the years and always maintained a friendly relationship with him. Vincente for his part, always held a distinct and special place in his heart for his first wife.

TOP Judy in London in April 1951.

After several very well-received appearances on radio, Judy accepted an invitation to appear in concert at The London Palladium, leaving for Europe by boat on March 30, 1951. Opening night at the Palladium was stupendous, (including the amusing tumble Judy took onstage as she tried to turn and exit; she burst into laughter and the audience joined in), and the entire four-week engagement was sold out soon after the box office opened the next morning. The London morning papers all proclaimed Judy's show a triumph. It was just what she needed to renew her faith in herself and her abilities as a performer. Judy's tour was extended to include appearances in Scotland and Ireland, the land of her grandparents, where she was met with much affection and superlative notices. In Scotland she told the audience, "I'm Scots-Irish, you know," and regaled the crowds with show business stories and family stories, as well as invited several youngsters on stage to join her in an impromptu Highland Fling. Said the Irish Press, "Judy Garland turned a formal concert into an intimate singsong house party with 3500! The audience adored her and would have carried her on their shoulders out of the theatre and down the Royal Mile if she had allowed it."

BOTTOM Danny Kaye plants a big kiss on Judy's cheek following their appearances in the All-Star Midnight Sid Field (an old-time comedian) Tribute at the London Palladium. Other stars at the tribute included Orson Welles, Vivien Leigh and Laurence Olivier.

Just a few weeks prior to leaving for London, Judy had met a gentleman by the name of Michael Sidney Luft. They dated for a few weeks before Judy left for Great Britain, then Sid surprised Judy with his arrival in London. Judy asked Sid to take over her career as manager and Sid put together a grand tour of the British Isles. Judy and Sid were soon a regular Hollywood couple, seen at all the requisite clubs and gatherings including one where Gloria DeHaven (bottom) tried to convince Judy to have special apliques applied to her nails and hands, then a hot fashion trend. (Judy seems unconvinced.)

TOP The Palace marquee
BOTTOM Judy arriving at the Palace with Sid Luft

After the British tour, Judy, accompanied by Sid Luft, returned to the United States eager to put together the same concert tour in their home country. Sid worked out a deal with the owners of the Palace Theatre in New York City, once the most famous theatre in the world, in which the theatre was to be completely redone, reviving its past grandeur and elegance, and for Judy to be its grand reopening act.

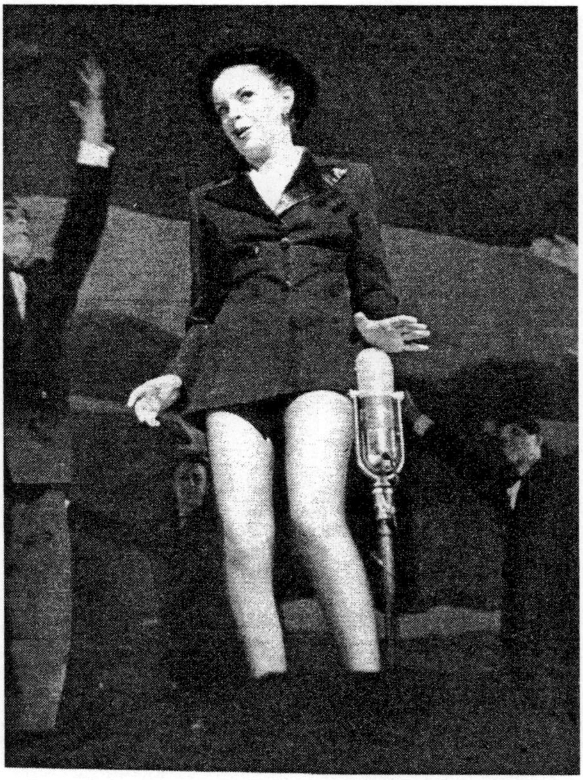

"I'll sing'em all, and we'll stay all night."

- Judy Garland during a NYC concert appearance

Opening at The Palace Theatre in New York City on October 16, 1951, Judy offered the audience more than two hours of song, dance and, most of all, personal contact. Judy's live performances always featured a tremendous amount of warmth and interaction between the star and her audience, whom she called her "friends." Judy chatted, joked and reminisced. The morning papers proclaimed Judy's Palace performance unequaled, comparing it in sensation to such historical events as Lindbergh's solo flight and the end of World War I.

TOP Judy leaving the Palace after her opening night.

As Judy prepared to leave the Palace on opening night, she was advised that thousands of her fans were waiting for her in front of the theatre and that she should leave through a back exit in order to avoid the mob. Judy refused. Instead, she donned a marvelous evening gown and marched straight through the main lobby and greeted her fans. This was to become an almost nightly ritual during the Palace engagement, one which accurately demonstrates the mutual, love and respect that Judy and her fans shared.

BOTTOM December 31, 1951. Judy and Sid Luft celebrate the dawning of 1952 at the Sherry Netherlands Hotel in New York.

TOP Judy's amazing run at the Palace was punctuated with nightly attendance by the biggest names of the time, from foreign dignitaries to national politicians to popular celebrities. All wanted to be witness to the entertainment history being made on Broadway in 1951. Here, fellow former MGM star Elizabeth Taylor and then rising star Montgomery Clift pay homage to Judy backstage.

BOTTOM Closing night at the Palace on February 24, 1952. Judy's Palace engagement closed with just as much fanfare as that with which it had opened. Judy did numerous encores until finally she called upon the audience to supply the very last song of the engagement. While standing on stage in her very comfortable robe and slippers, the audience serenaded Judy with "Auld Lang Syne," bringing her - and everyone else - to tears. Judy engagement had brought in $800,000 in receipts, equal today to about six million dollars.

TOP On March 31 1952, Judy, along with Yul Brynner, Gertrude Lawrence and Phil Silvers were awarded Antoinette Perry Awards (known popularly as the "Tony") at the Theatre Wing's sixth annual ceremony at the Waldorf- Astoria Hotel in New York City. Judy received the specially prepared Tony for her "important contribution to the revival of vaudeville." Pictured with the award recipients is Helen Hayes.

BOTTOM After the Palace engagement ended, Judy and manager Sid Luft were married. In April, Judy had a spectacular appearance at The Los Angeles Philharmonic and was congratulated by many former MGM friends including Mervyn LeRoy. That June, Judy was honored by The Friars Club, being dubbed "Miss Show Business."

THIS PAGE The funeral of Judy's mother, Ethel Gumm, January 8, 1953. Judy is seen arriving and leaving from the funeral with her husband Sid Luft, sister Sue Cathcart and family friend and business associate, Vernon Alves.

In January 1953, Judy was devastated by the sudden death of her mother, Ethel Gumm. Judy and her mother had been experiencing an up and down relationship for about eighteen months previous, but had just begun a reconciliation when Ethel passed away. Judy, with her sisters, arranged for their mother's funeral, then retired for several weeks of rest under her doctor's care. While stories of other stars' mothers, including those of Shirley Temple, Jean Harlow, Jane Withers and Elizabeth Taylor, make note of these women as engaging in such classic stage mother behavior as standing behind directors giving orders, or putting their daughter through unheard of situations, it is interesting to note that no one has ever presented or given witness to any incident of Ethel Gumm ever acting as such towards Judy or either of her older daughters.

TOP Judy often donated her services to charity, especially those involved with providing for care and services for children. Here she appears at a benefit for The American Cancer Society, with Milton Berle, Walter Winchell and Sugar Ray Robinson. Judy also worked for Easter Seals, as well as for numerous organizations that helped the physically challenged.

BOTTOM Judy gives a kiss to the poster child for the March of Dimes, an organization for which she worked since a teen star at MGM. Also pictured is the wife of General Douglas MacArthur.

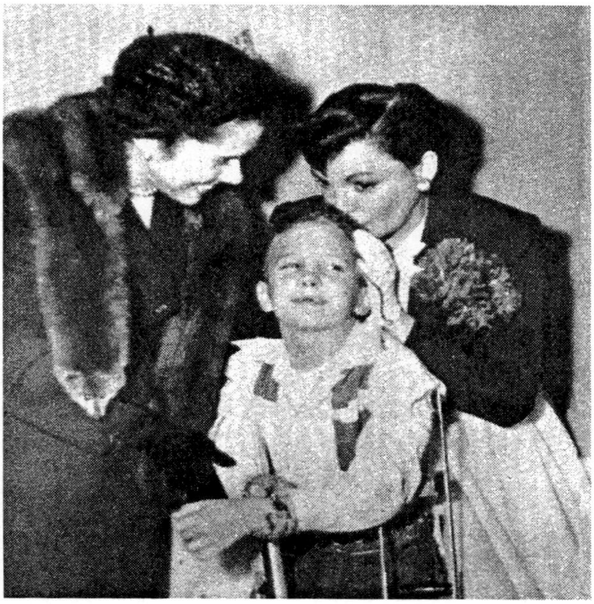

TOP First day of production on *A Star is Born* in October 1953 with diretcor George Cukor and Warner studio boss Jack Warner, Steve Trilling, Bill Orr and Winton Hoch.

BOTTOM Judy shares a laugh with assistant dance director Jack Harmon, and costume designer Irene Sharaff. *A Star is Born* was made by Warner Borthers in conjunction Transcona Enterprises, a new movie production company formed by Judy and Sid Luft. *Star* was the only film that Transcona ever produced.

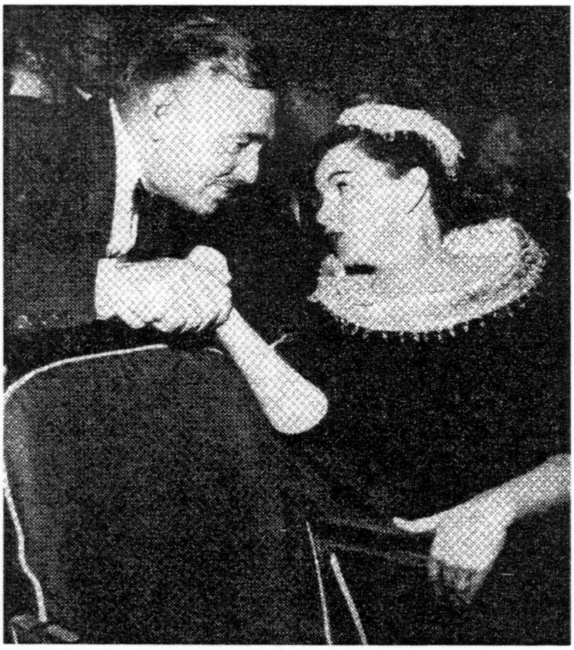

TOP At the September 30, 1954 Hollywood premiere of *A Star is Born* Clark Gable couldn't hide his affection for his old gal.

BOTTOM Judy and Sid Luft are surrounded by crowds as they arrive for the New York City premiere of *A Star is Born*.

Warner Bros. had put out a press release stating that *Star* was Judy's first film for their studio. "Not so!" cried WB assistant Mecca Graham. Graham, a lifelong Warner employee, recalled that one of his first assignments with the studio was on a series of juvenile shorts, a few of which featured Judy and her sisters. Warner Bros. immediately searched for the vintage films and when found, a special screening was held of the films. According to columnist Howard McClay, Judy loved seeing the films, but could not recall making them. "I was only about seven then, so how could I possibly remember them. Besides, this film debut was rather inauspicious, so it wouldn't stick in my memory. But I'm thrilled to have found a forgotten memento of a very pleasant experience."

TOP At the Hollywood Foreign Correspondents Awards Dinner (popularly known as the Golden Globes) on February 24 1955, Judy accepted accolades for *A Star is Born,* along with fellow award recipients, Marlon Brando, who won for *On the Waterfront* and Edmund O'Brien, who won for *The Barefoot Contessa*.

BOTTOM On March 8, 1955, LOOK magazine feted a very pregnant Judy as Best Actress for her role in *A Star is Born,* along with Bing Crosby as Best Actor for *The Country Girl*. Red Skelton presented the awards on his then v ery popular television show. Both Judy and Bing would be nominated as Best Actor and Actress by the Academy of Arts and Sciences, but neither would go on to win the Oscar.

TOP After *A Star is Born*, Judy returned to the live stage. On July 12, 1955 she appeared in concert at The Long Beach Municipal Auditorium in a performance attended by most of her friends, all of whom just happened to be the biggest names in Hollywood at the time. Frank Sinatra co-ordinated the event, sending invitations that read "For Our Judy," chartering a bus to bring such stars as Humphrey Bogart, Lauren Bacall, Debbie Reynolds, Eddie Fisher, and Betty Hutton to the show, as well as arranging for special security.

BOTTOM Judy takes to the mike at the Long Beach performance.

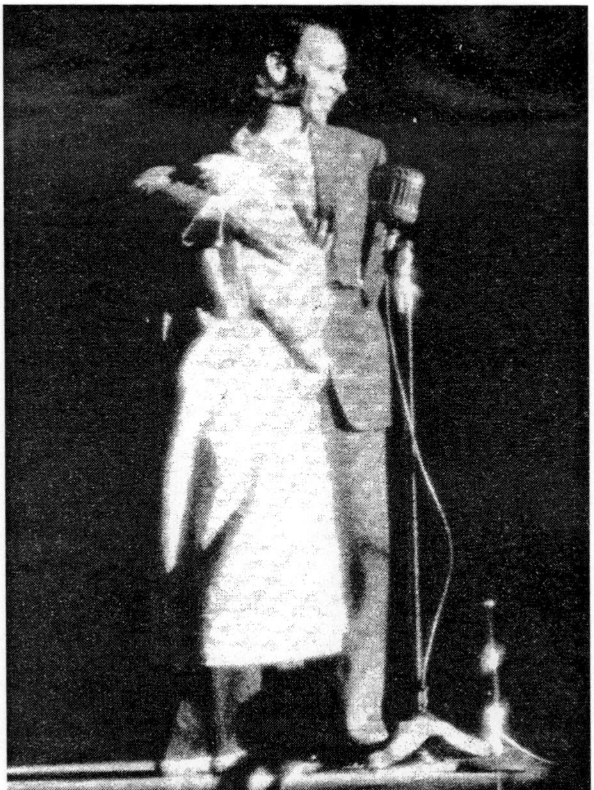

TOP After Judy took her encores and headed backstage, the group took to the stage, brought their girl out in her bathrobe and slippers and put on a whole new show of song, dance and jokes for the audience. (l to r) Dean Martin, Sammy Davis, Jr., Sid Luft, Mike Romanoff, David Wayne, Edger Bergan, Judy.

BOTTOM After her show, Judy asked Sinatra to sing. Frank declined pointing to Judy and declaring, "How could anyone follow this?"

TOP Judy made her television debut on September 24, 1955 on the premiere of "Ford Star Jubilee" on the CBS network. Although rehearsals had gone very well, Judy awoke the morning of the live show with a case of laryngitis. Ever the trouper, Judy went on with the program, bounding off stage in-between songs in order to have her throat treated.

BOTTOM Judy with David Wayne who joined her on television for her traditional tramp finale. Judy's performance was well-received by television audiences and viewers jammed the CBS switchboards with calls asking to see more of the star on television. Excited by all of this adulation, CBS offered Judy a long-term contract for three more television specials. The network also purchased the television broadcast rights to *The Wizard of Oz.* For the first time in broadcast history, the movie was shown on television the following November 1956 with Judy hosting the event. It was a huge success and a beloved television tradition had begun.

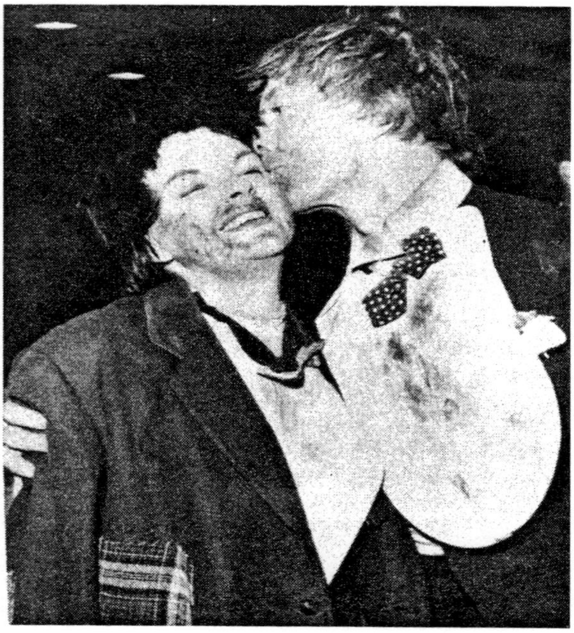

TOP June 9, 1955. Judy with Noel Coward, British dramatist and actor, and Lauren Bacall. Coward was appearing in Las Vegas at the Desert Inn.

MIDDLE Are Judy and Mickey getting ready "to put on a show" in November 1955?

BOTTOM Judy, Sid Luft and Kirk Douglas.

TOP Judy runs through a gauntlet of cheering fans as she races to be on time for the premiere of *The Man with The Golden Arm* in 1955.

BOTTOM Famed Hollywood columnist Louella Parson corners Judy and husband Sid Luft at a tinseltown event.

TOP During the summer of 1956 Judy had made her Las Vegas debut at The New Frontier Hotel. Judy then returned to New York's Palace Theatre for a second sensational engagement in late 1956. On December 1, 1956, Judy was honored on stage after her performance by The Troupers, a female theatrical and charitable organization.

BOTTOM Judy and her 1956 Palace musical director, Jack Cathcart, who was also her brother-in-law, the husband of Judy's eldest sister, Susanne.

"I love to sing and I love to make people as happy as I am."

- Judy Garland

TOP Judy takes a breather while recording at Capitol Records.

BOTTOM Judy and Dinah Sore.

In early 1957, Judy became embroiled in a messy court case involving a reporter from a NY newspaper. The reporter ran a column in which she quoted some nasty remarks made by CBS-TV executives, who were less than satisfied with their working relationship with Judy. Judy sued CBS and the court requested that the reporter reveal her sources for the quotes. She steadfastly refused causing the court to send her to jail for contempt. Because the reporter was also a young mother with several children, newspapers had a field day with headlines screaming that Judy Garland had imprisoned a young mother. It is interesting to note, however, that both Judy and the reporter agreed that it all could have been avoided had the CBS-TV executives involved had the character and integrity to come forth themselves.

TOP In October 1957, Judy returned to London, appearing for just over four weeks at the Palladium and Dominion theatres. Judy always expressed great fondness for London, saying, (in reference to her first concert appearances after leaving MGM at the London Palladium in 1951), "London gave me back my faith in myself." Judy is shown with musical director Gordon Jenkins at an October 15th rehearsal.

MIDDLE Alan King performed with Judy both in the United States and in London. King has alway had nothing but praise and admiration for Judy, calling his time working with her among "the best years of my life."

BOTTOM While at a rehearsal for a Palladium show on November 17, Judy strikes her trademark concert pose; pouring out a number while perched on the edge of the stage.

"I've always liked the spotlight, I'm afraid. I've always felt at home in it, like sitting by the fireside, all cozy."

- Judy Garland

ABOVE Judy and her "boyfriends" at the Dominion Theatre in London.

Selling-out the three thousand seat theatre on a nightly basis, Judy received nothing but tremendous acclaim throughout the Dominion engagement, ending in a triumphant closing night that featured an encore performance (next page) of her "A Couple of Swells" routine. A few days after the Dominion engagement, Judy appeared in performance before the British Royal Family. Although several other famous performers had been called to entertain the Queen, the press, it seemed, only had room in their hearts - and reviews - for Judy, calling the evening, "Judy Garland's Night." After the show, Judy was presented to Queen Elizabeth II.

TOP Judy takes her bows closing night at the Dominion.

BOTTOM Judy is surrounded by fans and floral tributes at London's Dominion Theatre in October 1957. Judy followed up her London appearances with a holiday engagement in Las Vegas. The Vegas stint started off well, but deteriorated rapidly due to Judy's intermittent bouts of laryngitis, coupled with a New Year's Eve crowd of raucous and rude revilers who provoked a few stressful moments. Immediately afterwards, Judy enjoyed a brief, but very necessary rest.

TOP In March 1958, Judy was appearing at Ben Maksik's Town and Country in Brooklyn, New York when she became ill with severe laryngitis, forcing her to pull out of her contract. The cancellation resulted in an ugly scene, amply detailed in newspapers after Judy gave a teary-eyed press conference about the event, then left New York to rest.

BOTTOM Judy bounced back quickly from the Brooklyn incident and appeared in concert on July 23, 1958 at The Cocoanut Grove in LA, the opening night of which was hailed as one of Judy's greatest live performances. (Laryngitis would once again settle in during this engagement, though seemingly not as bad as previous bouts.) Judy herself enjoyed the Grove event recalling her earliest experience there saying, "My mother would bring us to the famous tea dances they had and she would convince the conductor to let me sing and she would lead me to this very stage and say, 'Sing, baby.' "

"The rest of us will be forgotten, but never Judy."

- Frank Sinatra

ABOVE Judy clowns on stage at the Flamingo Hotel with Dean Martin and Frank Sinatra in late October/early November 1958.

Just prior to the above pictured Las Vegas engagement of November 1958, Judy had appeared in Chicago at Orchestra Hall. Judy's appearance at Orchestra Hall, a venue then known mainly for its classical music artists, raised a few eyebrows among the theatre's local well-heeled elitist patrons. After just a few minutes of her first evening's performance, however, any reservations as to Judy's suitability for the high-brow theatre were swept away by the cheers of the once again sell-out crowd.

"We lived in a white house with a garden. It's a beautiful, beautiful town. Grand Rapids is in the middle of the iron ranges of Minnesota, surrounded by lakes."

- Judy Garland on her birthplace

TOP Judy was very happy and proud to be able to take part in the centenary celebration of her home state of Minnesota during a brutally hot August 1958.

BOTTOM In May 1959, Judy appeared at New York City's Metropolitan Opera House, the first non-operatic performer ever to do so. Though her health had become increasingly problematic and some found her voice uneven at times, Judy received rave reviews. The week-long program brought in close to $200,000, equal today to just over 1.5 million dollars.

TOP After the success of her appearance at the Metropolitan Opera House, Judy proceeded to appear in concert at The War Memorial Opera House in Chicago (l) and at the San Francisco Opera House.

BOTTOM Judy, surrounded by flowers, collapses into a chair backstage at the War Memorial Opera House in Chicago. Judy is wearing her famous tramp costume, along with her equally famous smile. As soon as this tour of opera houses was complete, Judy departed first for L.A. (where she appeared at the Shrine Auditorium), then for New York City where she was hospitalized for some much needed rest, tests and medical attention.

Judy arriving in Amsterdam in December 1960.

7

The Beloved

Judy remained hospitalized in New York City through the holidays, receiving treatment for a badly inflamed liver and just plain exhaustion. As 1960 began, Judy's doctors had some unsettling news for her, for they were sure that, not only would she never be able to work again, but she probably had, at best, five years left to live. Although at first resigned to the idea of not working, Judy never believed for a minute that her time with her family, friends and fans was limited to only five more years and set about to prove the doctors wrong. In addition to live performances both in the United States and in Great Britain, Judy also appeared in the early 1960's in Paris and Amsterdam. Things at home, however, were less than happy as Judy filed for divorce from Sid Luft. The marriage had been experiencing highs and lows for several years, and this was just one of several breakups and patch-ups before the final 1965 divorce.

While Judy's marriage may have been crumbling, her movie career was on the upswing as she made four films between 1961 and 1962. After several successful concert tours and television appearances, Judy was afforded the opportunity to host her own television variety series for the CBS network. After the end of her television series, Judy took to the road once again, appearing in live performances and as a guest star on several popular variety and talk shows of the day. Many of the most famous Judy Garland stories of despair and disaster also took hold during this time, no matter how hard Judy tried to discount them. "I'd like to get something straight," she once told a reporter, "I do not cry. People are always writing that I'm bursting into tears. Well, the only thing I ever burst into is a song or a good yuck."

TOP Judy was still feeling a bit weak, but was much better than she had been, as she leaves Doctors' Hospital in New York City on January 5, 1960. Judy's first completed professional work of the new decade, was a recording of "Far Away Part of Town" for the soundtrack of the Columbia Pictures release, *Pepe*.

BOTTOM By April 1960, Judy was feeling and looking more like her old, exuberant self and successfully recorded a new album for Capitol Records.

TOP July 10, 1960. By the summer of 1960, Judy was once again healthy and ready to work. Here, Judy hits the campaign trail for Senator John F. Kennedy. Adlai Stevenson (l.), a twice defeated Democratic presidential candidate, poses for Sammy Davis, Jr., as a smiling Judy looks on during a fund-raiser/dinner on the eve of the Democratic National Convention. Just after the convention, Judy left for Europe where she appeared in August at the London Palladium.

BOTTOM Judy holds up a Kennedy poster as she entertains Americans living in Weisbaden, Germany at a Democratic rally on October 26th, 1960.

ABOVE In early October 1960, Judy made her Paris, France concert debut at the City of Light's Palais De Chaillot. Her performance received wide-acclaim by the French press and public alike. Flashing some high-powered smiles Judy's way are Maurice Chevalier (l.) and Anthony Perkins (c.) who were in the Paris audience. Amid the standing ovations, Chevalier congratulated Judy onstage after the performance.

TOP RIGHT Judy at a Capitol Records reception. Although Judy's first recordings independent of MGM were for Columbia Records, including the soundtrack to *A Star is Born*, her biggest recording success was with Capitol Records. Their association began in 1955 and ran through the mid-1960's.

BOTTOM Judy revealed a new dimension to her talent in 1961's *Judgement at Nuremberg* (directed in photo by Stanley Kramer) in which she tackled the very challenging- not to mention completely different from anything she had done previously - role of a German woman entangled in the Nazi atrocities of WWII. Judy's powerful portrayal was awarded with another Academy Award nomination, this time for Best Supporting Actress. Though Judy would ultimately lose the Oscar, she was honored in 1962 by the Hollywood Foreign Press Association (The Golden Globe Awards) with their annual Cecil B. DeMille Award for her contributions to entertainment.

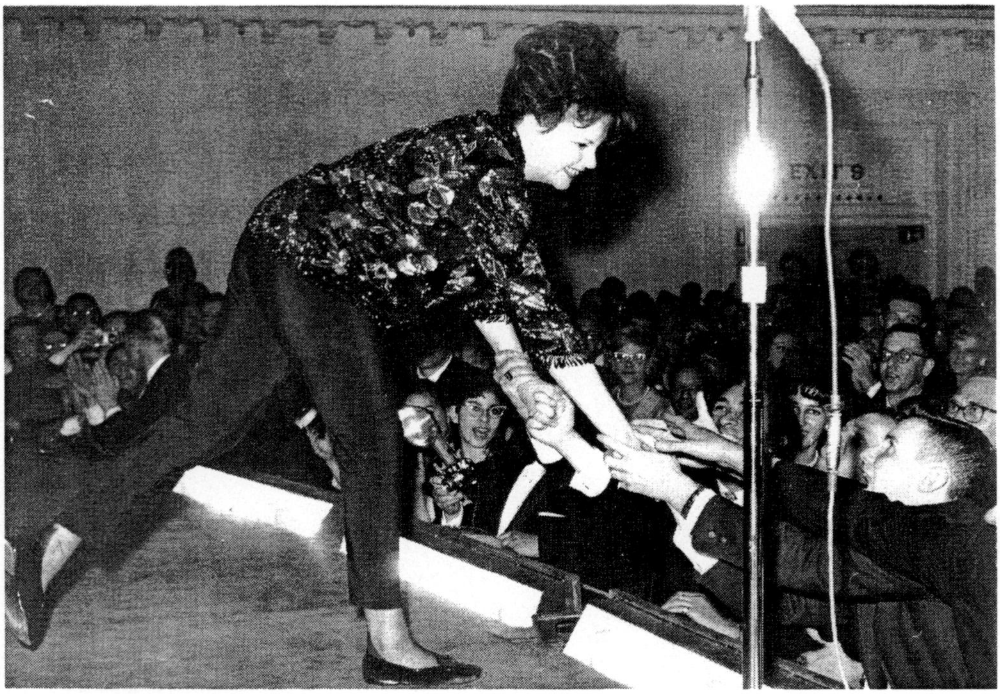

“I decided right away that they liked me, and I loved them, and we had ourselves a ball!”

- Judy Garland on her Carnegie Hall appearance.

During the first week of 1961, Judy began a nationwide concert tour that would hit thirty-one cities. Included in the list of appearances was an evening at New York City’s famed Carnegie Hall, the pinnacle of success for any musical performer. Come the appointed hour of 8pm on April 23, 1961, Judy was petrified. Carnegie Hall was filled to capacity with some of the biggest names in the world. As Judy took to the stage, her fears melted into the deafening din of applause, cheers, whoops and shouts. “I decided right away that they liked me and I loved them,” she told reporters, “and we had ourselves a ball!” Said Judy of the frenzy that almost always surrounded her live appearances, “I don’t know what it is, really. Maybe it’s because people sense that I feel so good and that I work so hard to please them. I love to sing and I love to make people as happy as I am, which is apparently pretty infectious. Beyond this, I don’t know what causes it.”

"I don't know what it is, really. Maybe it's because people sense that I feel so good and that I work so hard to please them. I love to sing and I love to make people as happy as I am, which is apparently pretty infectious."

- Judy Garland on the frenzy associated with her concerts

Judy arrives in curlers for her second Carnegie Hall concert performance on May 21, 1961. The first three hour performance (April 23) was recorded live by Capitol records and "Judy at Carnegie Hall" was released the following July. Within two weeks it sold over 100,000 copies and remains one of the all-time best selling recordings ever made. Winning five Grammy Awards, including one for Judy as Best Solo Female Vocal Performance, "Judy at Carnegie Hall" has never been out of print.

TOP A second television special, "The Judy Garland Show," aired February 25, 1962 and featured not only Judy, but also Frank Sinatra and Dean Martin. Consisting of little more than songs and some banter among the three, "The Judy Garland Show" was a huge success.

MIDDLE In early 1962, Judy dines with Frank Sinatra and Juliet Prowse.

BOTTOM Judy smiles as she leaves Carson-Tahoe Hospital on September 15, 1962 with her physician, Dr. Kermit Osserman, after an almost day-long stay. Judy was suffering from kidney stones, the result of a punishing, self-imposed month-long fast to lose weight. Although the ailment produced severe pain, Judy recovered quickly and went onto her next concert run at the Las Vegas Sahara. Judy's three-week engagement at the Las Vegas Sahara was so well-received that hotel management asked her stay on an additional two weeks, appearing nightly at a lively - and very well-attended - performance at 2:30 each morning.

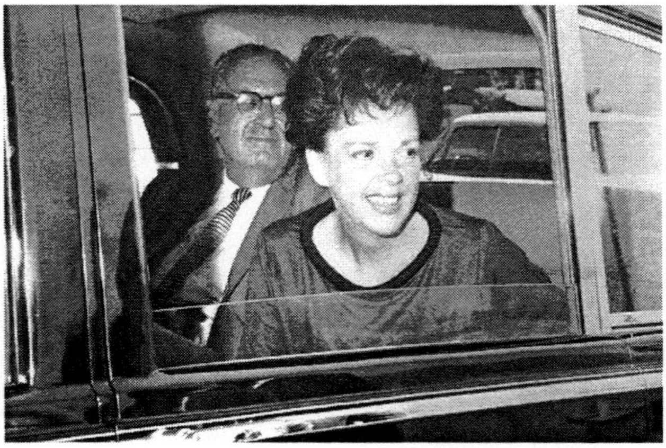

TOP Judy and Robert Goulet record the soundtrack to *Gay-Purr-ee*. The following November, Judy attended the Chicago premiere of *Gay Purr-ee*, a Warner Bros. animated feature for which she supplied the voice of "Mewsette," a cartoon kitty.

MIDDLE In December 1962, Judy appeared on "The Jack Paar Program." Her voice, her storytelling, her warmth and her wit won tremendous acclaim, and the idea for Judy's own television variety show took root. Initial taping began in June 1963. "The Judy Garland Show" debuted in September 1963, but would last only one season.

BOTTOM Just prior to the launch of her series, Judy appeared in another successful television special, this time with Phil Silvers and Robert Goulet.

TOP John Cassavetes directs Judy and child actor, Bruce Ritchie, in *A Child is Waiting,* released in January 1963. Judy starred in the film with Burt Lancaster.

MIDDLE Judy with Dirk Bogarde at the London premiere of their film *I Could Go on Singing* on March 7, 1963. This would ultimately be Judy's last completed film.

BOTTOM Richard Chamberlain, Judy Garland, and Mickey Rooney in September 1963. Chamberlin was starring in the hit television series "Dr. Kildare" in which he played the title role.

TOP August 1963. Judy was among several stars who headed up a Hollywood-based organization to support the fight for civil rights. With Judy are fellow lead members Charlton Heston, Eartha Kit, and Marlon Brando.

MIDDLE Judy and Maximilian Schell

BOTTOM Judy with Robert Goulet and Carol Lawrence.

TOP and BOTTOM Hong Kong June 1964.

After her formal separation from Sid Luft, Judy entered into a relationship with Mark Herron in early 1964. Herron accompanied Judy on a concert tour of Australia that started out well, but ended up in frustration and disappointment when Judy's initial triumphant performances deteriorated due to exhaustion and anxiety. Judy and Herron left Australia for Hong Kong where Judy became so ill that it was mistakenly reported that she had passed away. She was hospitalized but recovered quickly, and left the hospital after a few days without any assistance. It was during this time that Judy received news of the sudden death of her eldest sister, Susanne. It was initially reported that, upon learning her husband had left her for another woman, Susie had taken an overdose of sleeping pills, but a later investigation determined that she had actually passed away from a toxic reaction to a new medication just prescribed to her for a rare blood abnormality.

TOP While in Hong Kong, Judy was introduced to "The Allen Brothers," Peter (l.) and Chris, two non-related young singers. She immediately forged both a professional and personal relationship with them, signing them to open for her during her subsequent London engagement and afterward.

BOTTOM In November 1965, Judy married Mark Herron in Las Vegas. Here the couple arrange for their marriage license. Their union lasted less than five months.

TOP Judy had several successful television turns on such 1960s' favorites as "The Hollywood Palace," "The Ed Sullivan Show," and "The Andy Williams Show." Her performances during this time wavered anywhere between super and so-so, as did her sometimes erratic behavior, both of which were always the result of her increasingly delicate physical and emotional condition brought on by years of fluctuating weight, overwork, prescription medicine, less than supportive relationships and financial strain. But Judy pushed on, never once looking back at her detractors.

MIDDLE Judy fulfilled about a dozen concert dates between February and December 1965, including a September performance at LA's Greek Theatre. On the second day of the engagement, Judy fell and broke her arm. Although in much pain, she insisted upon going on with that night's show. Seated in a large armchair, Judy was aided on stage by friends including Mickey Rooney, Johnny Mathis and Martha Raye.

BOTTOM See next page.

BOTTOM LEFT March 2, 1967. Judy with author Jacqueline Susanne's best selling novel, "The Valley of the Dolls," the film version of which it was announced that Judy would star. The film was a daring, somewhat raunchy film for the times and, after Judy had time to realize exactly what the film was all about, she abruptly walked away from the project. Judy did not care that the press was reporting that she had been fired or that she had caused trouble on the set. It was worth it she said because, "I may not be Dorothy on my way to "Oz" anymore, but at least I'm not vulgar."

TOP Judy and Tony Bennett.

BOTTOM March 12, 1968. Judy and former *Wizard of Oz* co-star Ray Bolger reenacted a pose as "Dorothy" and "The Scarecrow" when Judy attended Bolger's engagement at The Empire Room in New York City. Bolger had the highest regard for Judy saying, "I had great admiration for Judy both as a person and a performer. She liked to have fun, but once the cameras were rolling she was serious and dedicated. You'll read stories about how difficult Judy became to work with, but I never saw any evidence of that and I made two pictures with her. She was always so respectful of her fellow performers and the technicians. We never had any problems with her."

TOP Along with five television appearances, Judy completed six concert appearances during 1968, including one as substitute host on "The Merv Griffin Show." Between June 1967 and December 1968, Judy completed more than twenty-one live performances including her last (triumphant) engagement at the Palace in New York City in July/August 1967.

RIGHT Judy left the United States for London in December of 1968. She had as her companion a young man named Mickey Deans. In between concerts in England, Sweden and Denmark, Judy and Mickey Deans were married that March of 1969 and settled down to life in Great Britain. Judy publicly proclaimed that she was looking forward to some rest before embarking on some new and exciting projects. But those projects would never come to pass. The world uttered a collective wail of sorrow as it was announced on Sunday, June 22, 1969 that Judy Garland had passed away in London from an accidental overdose of prescription sleeping aids. The coroner was adamant that there was no evidence of suicide, and that her body showed no signs alcoholism or liver disease as was widely reported. It is speculated that Judy had awakened during the night and, groggy and unable to return to sleep, had taken a second dosage of her prescription sleeping pills. Judy had dropped to less than 90 pounds during the previous year and, in its frail state, her body was simply unable to handle a second dose and the results proved fatal. Those who spoke with Judy the evening before said that she was in excellent spirits and gave no indication of any trouble or distress.

TOP and BOTTOM Judy with Mickey Deans in 1969.

More than 22,000 people filed past Judy's glass covered coffin at The Frank E. Campbell Funeral Home on Madison Avenue in New York City. After the Episcopal services held on June 27, Judy's casket was taken from the funeral home to her final resting place in Ferncliff Cemetery in Hartsdale, New York. She is remembered, respected and missed still today.

Judy and her children leave New York for California in December 1962.

8

The Mother

The films, the concerts, the shows, the fans, the press, the tours, the awards, the adulation; none of it meant more to Judy Garland than motherhood. "She was a fabulous mother," middle child Lorna Luft repeatedly states when interviewed. It is a sentiment often echoed by Judy's eldest child, Liza Minnelli, as well as by her youngest, Joseph Luft.

Simply put, Judy adored her children and took them almost everywhere with her. She involved her children in her life as much as possible. Beginning with the Palace Theatre engagement of 1956, Judy began to make her concerts a family event as she would often bring each of her children up on stage to either sing with or to them. During one show, a young Liza Minnelli demonstrated her talents as she danced to her mother's background singing of "Swanee," presenting audiences with a glimpse of what the future held for Judy's eldest child. Judy usually sang "Rockabye Your Baby" for her younger girl while she often sang "Happiness is Just a Thing Called Joe" to her baby son cradled on her lap or in her arms.

After the Carnegie Hall events in New York City, Judy appeared in several other northeast cities, then returned to spend the holidays with her children in the family's rented Westchester, NY home. Although clearly a busy woman, Judy was determined to include her children in her life as much as possible, often opting to take her offspring with her on tour. When the children were unable to accompany their mother on tour, Judy made certain to speak by phone with each of them at least once a day. Judy was also as much of a traditional mother as her schedule allowed her to be, one who attended school plays, drove her kids to school, babied them when they were ill and took part in their daily activities as much as possible. Judy is also remembered by her children as being the disciplinarian in the family, of insisting on good behavior and proper manners and, most of all, of showering them with much love and affection.

"I think Liza decided to be a dancer in the womb, she kicked so much."

- Judy Garland

ABOVE At a time when photos of pregnant women were rarely published, Judy was about four months along with her first child when she and husband Vincente were photographed outside of Ciro's in Hollywood in October 1946.

RIGHT Long before anyone ever heard of "Little Ricky," it was little Liza, born March 12, 1946, who was Hollywood's baby, her every turn being captured by magazines and newspapers alike. Said Judy in a 1947 interview that she and Vincente had considered naming a daughter "Candace," but chose "Liza," not only after the song of the same name that the couple loved, but also because she was afraid that people would not know how to spell or pronounce the name "Candace." A pretty amusing thought today, considering that Liza Minnelli has spent a good part of her own career reminding people how to spell and pronounce "Liza!"

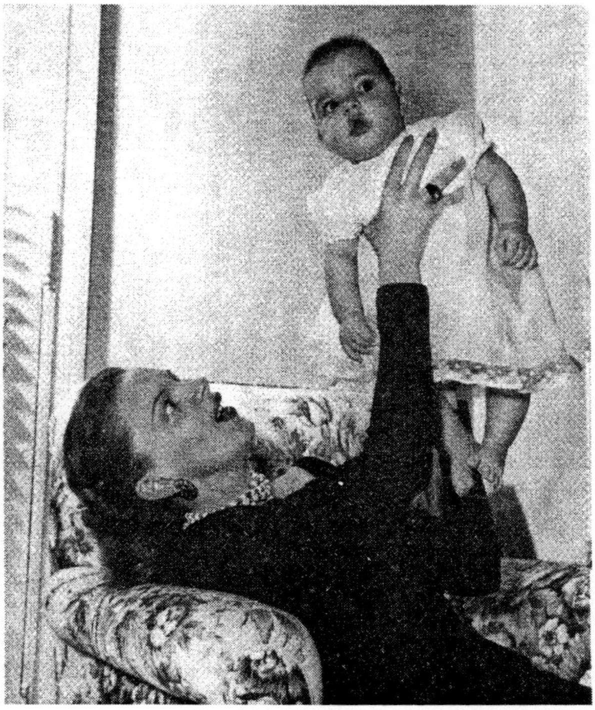

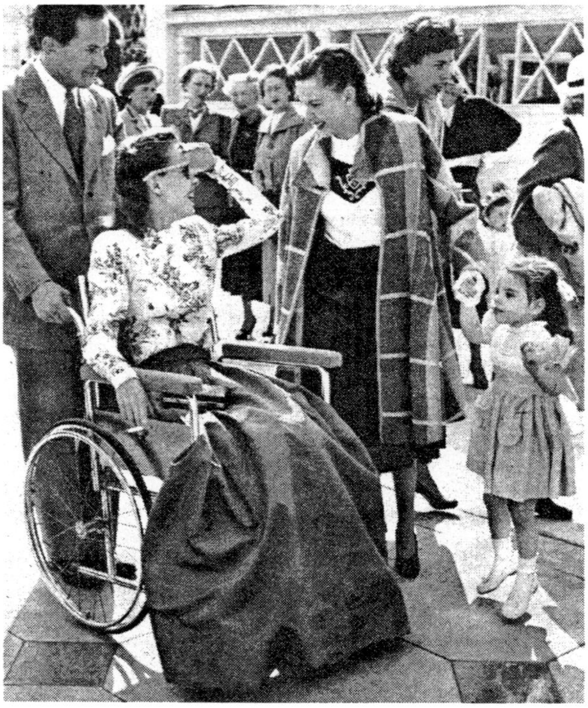

Judy holds tightly to the hand of a very excited three-year-old Liza as she talks with actress Susan Peters. (Peters was paralyzed in a 1945 hunting accident, but maintained a small acting career before passing away from varied health complications in 1952.) Judy and Liza were taking part in a March 1949 charity Easter event that featured egg hunts, basket weaving and, below, a visit from the original "Bozo the Clown." Liza clings tightly to Mama as Bozo tries to get up close and personal.

TOP Mother and Daughter in 1949.

BOTTOM June 1951. After Judy had been in London for a few weeks during her 1951 Palladium engagement, she sent for Liza who had been staying with her father in California. Previous to Liza's arrival, Judy had been spending thousands of dollars on transatlantic telephone calls to her daughter twice a day.

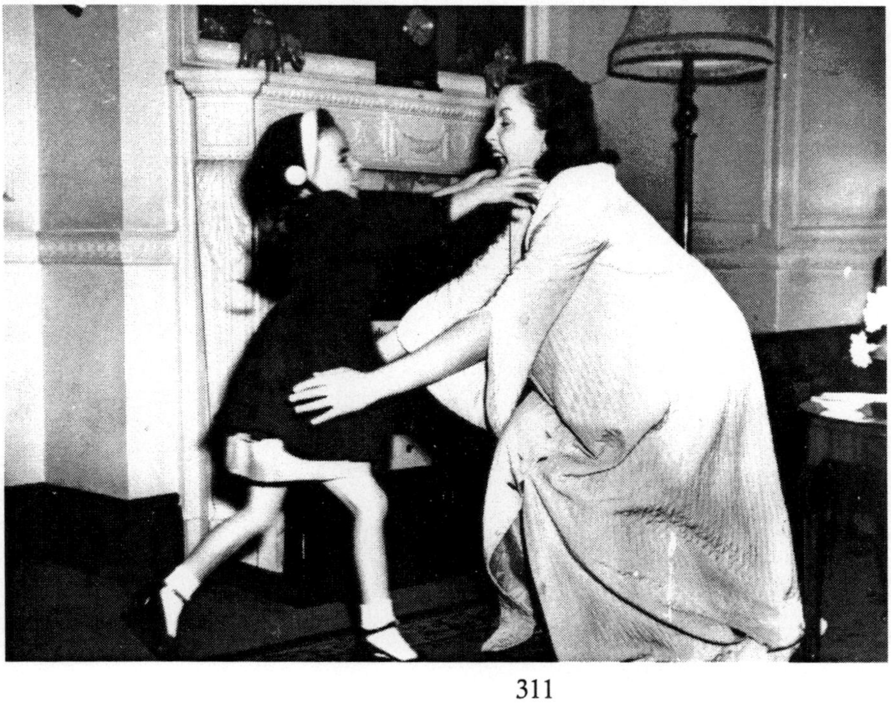

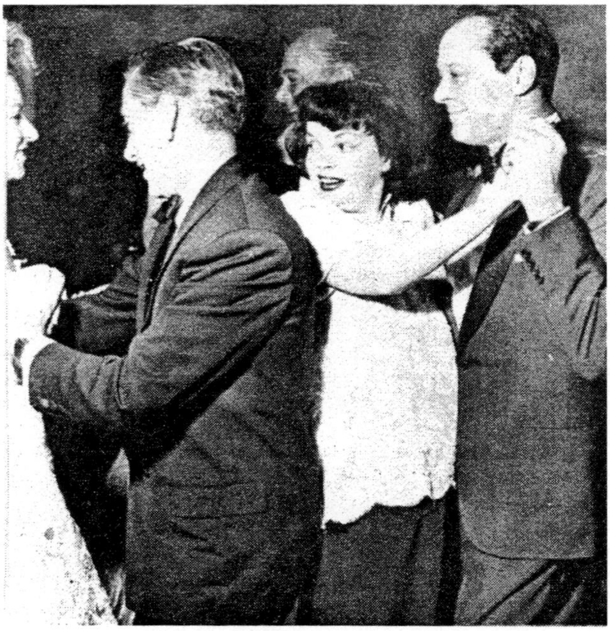

“I’ve always been happiest when I’m pregnant.”

- Judy Garland

Judy was photographed in her expectant state (top) on the dance floor with husband Sid Luft and (bottom) with actress Jane Wyman. Declared Judy, “I’m happiest when pregnant.”

"She was the most miraculous person to be around. Really an extraordinary person. Bright and funny and smart as a whip. And anything but tragic! She had such character, integrity, warmth and affection. It is a joy to talk about her. It always has been."

-Liza Minnelli

TOP Judy and her second child, Lorna, born on November 21, 1952.

BOTTOM Judy poses with her two girls on the set of *A Star is Born*. Lorna was about eighteen months and Liza, seven.

"God has already given me my own special 'Oscar,' my new baby son."

\- Judy Garland

Joseph Wiley Luft was born March 29, 1955, the night before the Academy Awards for 1954 were to be announced. The baby had been expected in late April, but an unexpected turn of events caused the early delivery. The media crowded into Judy's hospital room on the following evening of March 30th so that they could record her live reaction were she to win the Oscar for Best Actress for *A Star is Born*. Judy lost the award to Grace Kelly, but expressed only great happiness and gratitude saying, "God has already given me my own special 'Oscar,' my new son." Judy had wanted to name a son "Joshua," but according to the boy's father, "that sounded like a kid in an Eton suit and he offered the name "Joe" instead.

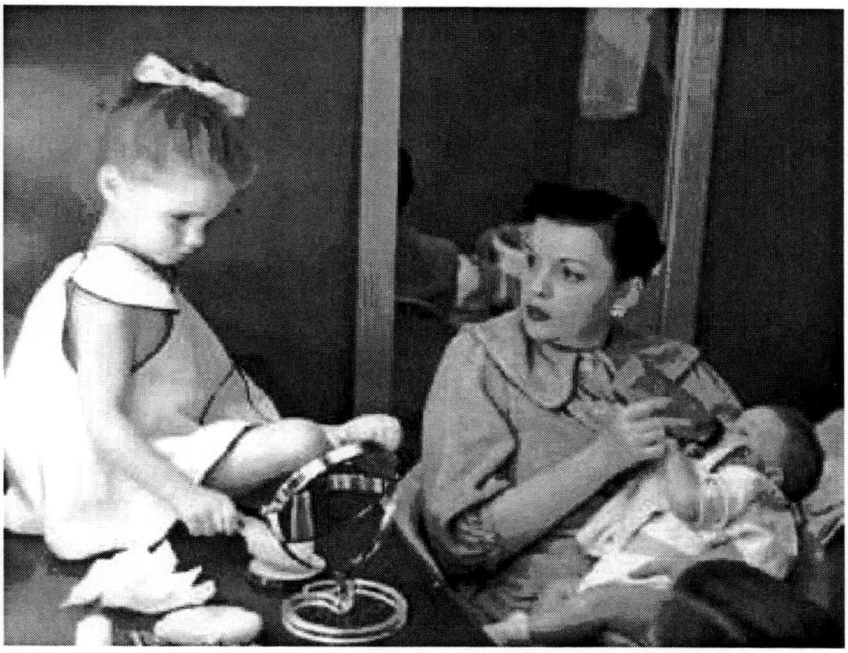

THIS PAGE Judy tends to Baby Joe's nutritional needs while keeping an eye on daughter Lorna, almost age three, and (bottom) takes time out of rehearsal to share a hug with nine-year-old Liza in mid-1955. Said Liza of her mother in a 2002 interview, "I have never had a horrifying family relationship with my mother. She was great to me. She was really the best." Added Lorna in a previous interview, "She was a fabulous mother."

"People would like to think that my mother was some tragic, unloved figure, but she wasn't. She was a fabulous mother."

-Lorna Luft

TOP and BOTTOM November 1960. Judy and the kids welcome a new member to the family in London.

BOTTOM Judy takes an almost eight-year-old Lorna and five-year-old Joe to bed at the Chelsea, London home they rented during the family's stay in the United Kingdom.

TOP Judy brings her children on stage at New York City's famed Carnegie Hall in 1961. Said Judy of her children, "They are the most important things in my life, far more important to me than my career or my success or anything else. They are all so friendly and open and sweet...a great joy!"

BOTTOM April 29, 1962. Judy and children arrive in London. Judy was to begin filming *I Could Go on Singing*. By this time, Judy and Sid Luft were separated with both seeking custody of their children.

“She was an incredible person...she was so full of life,”

-Joseph Luft

TOP Judy meets Liza at LA Airport in November 1963.Seventeen-year-old Liza Minnelli returned to California from NYC in order to work on her mother’s television series, receiving much favorable acclaim.Mother and daughter performed together, while Liza also offered a solo number.

MIDDLE The Judy Garland Christmas Show from 1963. Judy also featured Liza, Lorna and Joe in a special family Christmas episode of her variety series in which each of the children performed on a set designed to replicate the family’s home.

BOTTOM Judy and Liza rehearse for their only concert together at The London Palladium in November 1964. In London, Judy introduced Liza to Peter Allen, one half of the Allen Brothers duo that was now traveling with her. Liza and Peter would marry in 1967.

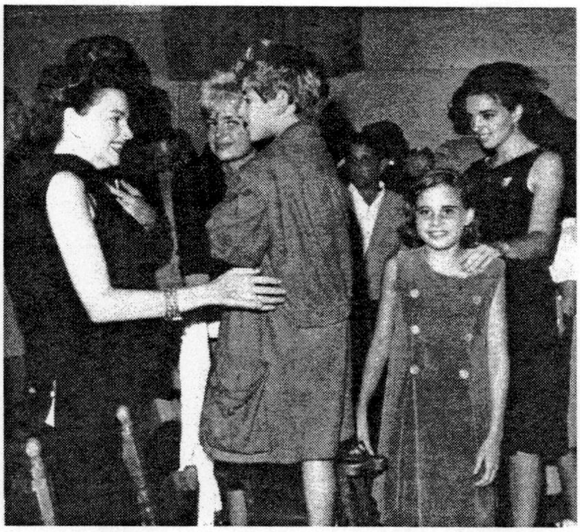

TOP Judy congratulates Joe and Lorna on their successful portrayal of "The Cowardly Lion" and "Dorothy" in their 1963 elementary school production of *The Wizard of Oz*. Despite her demanding schedule, Judy tried hard to be as much of a traditional mother as she could be. "When she would drive us to school," recalled Lorna Luft in a recent interview, "she would teach us songs in the car and she was a wonderful teacher- terrible driver. She'd be teaching a song, and we'd be weaving all over the road. It was great."

MIDDLE December 29, 1964.
Judy and Liza meet Lorna and Joe at Kennedy Airport in New York City. Judy's younger children had just arrived from California. Said Judy of the manner in which she was bringing up her children, "I'm a strict disciplinarian at home. For one thing, I'm a fiend about good manners. I may be strict, but my kids aren't afraid of me. We respect each other, as well as enjoy each other."

BOTTOM December 30, 1964. Judy's kids visit with Carol Channing backstage at *Hello, Dolly*.

"They are the most important things in my life, far more important to me than my career or my success or anything else. They are all so friendly and open and sweet...a great joy!" - Judy Garland on her children

LEFT Judy's greatest joy was found in her children, whether it be with Lorna and Joe at Disney Land or congratulating Liza at her opening night at The Cocoanut Grove.

THIS PAGE In July/August1967, Judy appeared in concert in six cities including an engagement at The Palace Theatre in New York City, her third appearance there. Lorna and Joe were featured as part of this tour, with Lorna offering several songs and Joe taking a turn on the drums. Mama, Lorna and Joe also performed together.

ABOVE Judy's three children, Joe Luft, Lorna Luft and Liza Minnelli circa 1985.

While Joe Luft enjoys a non public-oriented lifestyle, both Liza Minnelli and Lorna Luft have followed the family tradition as professional entertainers. Lorna Luft is the mother of a son and daughter.

In the years following Judy Garland's death, numerous books, documentaries and magazine articles have sought to provide readers with information on the beloved star. Most of this material, however, has been sensationalized so as to overshadow the many happy and heartwarming aspects of Judy's life and career. Much of the information disseminated about Judy after her passing eagerly embraced gossip, speculation and personal opinion as fact. Events and circumstances were misconstrued in order to further an image of Judy as "tragic victim," a characterization that she herself consistently denied and lampooned during her last years.

It must also be remembered that Judy suffered through her greatest trials during a time when the effects of medication, prescription or otherwise, were not completely understood, nor were there available any of the support and treatment centers that are today so commonplace. As such, Judy's down periods were never presented, either at the time they were occurring or afterward, in the proper light.

Judy's children have tried hard to make people understand that she was unlike much of what the published reports and broadcasts would like people to believe, that, despite many daunting challenges and unfortunate circumstances, she was a profoundly loving, funny, warm, kind and very happy person. "She was an incredible person...she was so full of life," said son Joe Luft in an interview. "She was a wonderful mother, absolutely wonderful," Liza Minnelli also emphatically declared in a recent interview. "She was the most miraculous person to be around. Really an extraordinary person. Bright and funny and smart as a whip. And anything but tragic! She had such character, integrity, warmth and affection. It is a joy to talk about her. It always has been." Added Lorna Luft in a separate interview, "There are so many myths, half-truths and lies out there about my mother. People would like to think that my mother was some tragic, unloved figure, but she wasn't. She was a fabulous mother."

Judy herself never seemed bothered by the tragic image the press created. She would shrug her shoulders, point to herself and say, "Anything that anybody says about this star over here, you can't stop them. They like what they read, what they write. It doesn't matter what they say. That stuff is going to build on its own. That has nothing to do with me. What has to do with me is my family, my children and my life...that we love together and stay together. That other stuff...I don't try to fight it. It's a losing battle.

"They just don't want to know the truth about the real woman."

Judy Garland in Films

The following are Judy's screen appearances, both feature length and short subject, including several she completed with her sisters. Also indicated is the studio for which the project was made, the year of release and the character Judy played.

Starlet Review (aka The Big Revue)	Meglin Kiddies short	1929	(The Gumm Sisters)
A Holiday in Storyland	Vitaphone short	1929	(The Gumm Sisters)
The Wedding of Jack and Jill	Vitaphone short	1929	(The Gumm Sisters)
Bubbles	Vitaphone short	1929	(The Gumm Sisters)
La Fiesta de Santa Barbara	MGM short	1935	(The Garland Sisters)
Every Sunday (Afternoon)	MGM short	1936	(Judy)
Pigskin Parade Fox	FOX	1936	(Sairy Dodd)
Broadway Melody of 1938	MGM	1937	(Betty Clayton)
Thoroughbreds Don't Cry	MGM	1937	(Cricket West)
Silent Night	MGM short	1937	(Herself)
Everybody Sing	MGM	1938	(Judy Bellaire)
Love Finds Andy Hardy	MGM	1938	(Betsy Booth)
Listen, Darling	MGM	1938	(Pinkie Wingate)
The Wizard of Oz	MGM	1939	(Dorothy Gale)
Babes in Arms	MGM	1939	(Patsy Barton)
If I Forget You	MGM short	1940	(Herself)
Andy Hardy Meets Debutante	MGM	1940	(Betsy Booth)
Strike Up the Band	MGM	1940	(Mary Holden)
Little Nellie Kelly	MGM	1940	(NellieKelly/Little Nellie)
Ziegfeld Girl	MGM	1941	(Susan Gallagher)
Life Begins for Andy Hardy	MGM	1941	(Betsy Booth)
Babes on Broadway	MGM	1941	(Penny Morris)
We Must Have Music	MGM short	1941	(Herself)
For Me and My Gal	MGM	1942	(Jo Hayden)

Presenting Lily Mars	MGM	1943	(Lily Mars)
Girl Crazy	MGM	1943	(Ginger Gray)
Thousands Cheer	MGM	1943	(Herself)
Meet Me in St. Louis	MGM	1944	(Esther Smith)
The Clock	MGM	1945	(Alice Maybery)
The Harvey Girls	MGM	1946	(Susan Bradley)
Ziegfeld Follies of 1946	MGM	1946	("The Star")
The Pirate	MGM	1948	(Manuela Alva)
Easter Parade	MGM	1948	(Hannah Brown)
Words and Music	MGM	1948	(Herself)
In the Good Old Summertime	MGM	1949	(Veronica Fisher)
Summer Stock	MGM	1950	(Jane Falbury)
A Star Is Born	Warner Bros	1954	(Esther/Vicki)
Pepe	Columbia	1960	(Soundtrack performance)
Judgment at Nuremberg	UA	1961	(Irene Hoffman)
Gay Purr-ee	Warner Bros	1963	(voice of Mewsette)
A Child Is Waiting	UA	1963	(Jean Hansen)
I Could Go On Singing	UA	1963	(Jenny Bowman)

Judy Garland in Concert

The following lists the dates and cities of most of Judy's concert appearances, although others may exist. Most of these dates represent multi-performaces lasting anywhere from one performance on one night, to two performances each day for six months.

1943 07/09 - Philadelphia, PA

1951 04/09 - London, England
05/21 - Glasgow, Scotland
05/29 - Edinburgh, Scotland
06/25 - London, England
07/01 - Dublin, Ireland
07/09 - Birmingham, England
10/16 - New York, NY

1952 04/21 - Los Angeles, CA
05/26 - San Francisco, CA

1953 04/29 - Lexington, KY

1955 07/08 - San Diego, CA
07/11 - Long Beach, CA
07/14 - Eugene, OR
07/15 - Portland, OR
07/17 - Seattle, WA
07/19 - Vancouver, BC
07/21 - Spokane, WA

1956 07/16 - Las Vegas, NV
09/26 - New York, NY

1957 05/01 - Las Vegas, NV
05/30 - Detroit, MI
06/10 - Dallas, TX
09/16 - Washington, DC
09/26 - Philadelphia PA
10/16 - London, England
11/19 - London, England
12/26 - Las Vegas, NV

1958 03/26 - Brooklyn, NY
07/23 - Los Angeles, CA
09/04 - Chicago, IL
10/01 - Las Vegas, NV

1959 02/07 - Miami, FL
04/27 - Baltimore, MD
05/11 - New York, NY
06/01 - Chicago, IL
07/01 - San Francisco, CA

1960 07/10 - Chicago, IL
07/16 - Los Angeles
08/28 - London, England
10/05 - Paris, France
10/26 - Wiesbaden, Germany

1960	10/28 - Paris, France
	12/01 - London, England
	12/10 - Amsterdam, Holland
1961	01/09 - Miami, FL
	02/21 - Dallas, TX
	02/23 - Houston, TX
	04/06 - Buffalo, NY
	04/11 - Birmingham, AL
	04/13 - Atlanta, GA
	04/15 - Charlotte, NC
	04/17 - Greensboro, NC
	04/23 - New York, NY
	04/30 - Philadelphia, PA
	05/02 - Newark, NJ
	05/06 - Chicago, IL
	05/08 - Dallas, TX
	05/10 - Houston, TX
	05/12 - Detroit, MI
	05/14 - Cleveland, OH
	05/21 - New York, NY
	07/01 - Queens, NY
	07/04 - New Port, RI
	08/04 - Atlantic City, NJ
	09/13 - San Francisco, CA
	09/16 - Los Angeles, CA
	09/20 - Denver, CO
	09/29 - White Plains, NY
	10/01 - Hartford, CT
	10/17 - Rochester, NY
1961 -	cont.
	10/19 - Pittsburgh, PA
	10/27 - Boston, MA
	10/29 - Montreal, Canada
	12/03 -Toronto, Canada
	12/09 - Washington, DC
1962	02/07 - Las Vegas, NV
	04/26 - New York, NY
	09/17 - Las Vegas, NV
	11/07 - Chicago, IL
1964	05/13 - Sydney, Australia
	05/20 - Melbourne, Australia
	11/09 - London, England
1965	02/08 - Toronto, Canada
	03/11 - Miami, FL
	05/07 - Chicago, IL
	05/22 - Charlotte, NC
	05/29 - Cincinnati, OH
	06/15 - Las Vegas, NV
	07/17 - Forest Hills, NY
	08/31 - San Carlos, CA
	09/13 - Los Angeles, CA
	11/30 - Las Vegas, NV
	12/17 - Houston, TX
1966	02/02 - Hollywood, FL
	08/17 - Mexico City, Mexico

1967 06/13 - Westbury, NY

06/26 - Springfield, MA

07/10 - Camden, NJ

07/31 - New York, NY

08/31 - Boston, MA

09/08 - Columbia, MD

09/14 - Chicago, IL

09/27 - St. Louis, MO

09/29 - Detroit, MI

10/01 - Indianapolis, IN

10/08 - Columbus, OH

10/20 - Hartford, CT

11/03 - South Orange, NJ

11/29 - Las Vegas, NV

12/26 - New York, NY

1968 02/18 - Baltimore, MD

02/25 - New York, NY

05/24 - Boston, MA

06/25 - Holmdale, NJ

07/20 - Philadelphia, PA

12/30 -London, England

1969 01/04 - London England

02/19 - London, England

03/19 - Stockholm, Sweden

03/23 - Malmo, Sweden

03/25 - Copenhagen, Denmark

Judy Garland on Television

The following lists Judy's television appearances, although a few others may exist.

1954 09/29 The Tonight Show

1955 09/24 The Ford Star Jubilee

12/26 The Tonight Show

1956 04/08 The Judy Garland Show (First TV Special)

11/03 The first television airing of *The Wizard of Oz*

1962 02/25 The Judy Garland Show (Second TV Special)

12/07 The Jack Paar Show

1963 03/1 Sunday Night at the Palladium (London)

03/19 Judy and Her Guests (Third Television Special)

04/19 The Ed Sullivan Show

1963 The Judy Garland Show aired weekly on Sunday evenings on CBS from September 1963 until March 1964

1964 12/11 The Jack Paar Show (London)

1965 02/05 On Broadway Tonight

04/05 The Academy Awards Show

09/13 The Gypsy Rose Lee Show

09/20 The Andy Williams Show

10/03 The Ed Sullivan Show

10/17 The Hollywood Palace

1966 02/28 The Kraft Music Hall

03/18 The Sammy Davis Jr

03/25 The Sammy Davis Jr

04/01 The Hollywood Palace

1967 03/05 What's My Line?

(Judy appeared on this popular 1960's game show during which her own voice was not used as the panelists would easily have known who it was. Instead, Judy used a bell/buzzer system to answer "yes" or "no" to the panelists' questions as they tried to decipher her identity.)

03/16 The Today Show

05/16 The Jack Paar Show

1968 06/24 The Tonight Show

07/18 The Mike Douglas Show

12/13 The Dick Cavett Show

12/17 The Tonight Show

12/19 The Merv Griffin Show

12/23 The Merv Griffin Show (Acted as hostess)

1969 02/19 Sunday Night at the Palladium (London)

For additional information on Judy's recordings and radio appearances, as well as a in depth biography of her life from 1922 until 1950 featuring more than 600 rare images, see *Judy Garland, The Golden Years* by Rita E. Piro. More information is available at www.judybook.com

Notes

Over the last thirty-two plus years, Judy Garland's life and career have been chronicled in more than 30 books as well as in countless periodicals, newspapers, websites, documentaries and more. The following is a listing of *some* of the resources that figured into the text of this publication. Numerous articles, documentaries, interviews, etc. were also referenced. If more information concerning a specific source or reference is desired, please contact us at judybook@judybook.com.

Books:

Dahl, David, and Kehoe, Barry: Young Judy

Finch, Christopher: Rainbow

Frank, Gerold: Judy

Fricke, J., J. Scarfone & Will. Stillman: The Wizard of Oz: The Official 50th Anniversary History

Hopper, Hedda: The Whole Truth and Nothing But

Minnelli, Vincente (Arce): I Remember it Well

Morella, Joe & Epstein, Edward: Judy: The Films & Career of Judy Garland

Rooney, Mickey: Life is Too Short

Scarfone, J. & Stillman, W.: The Wizardry of Oz

St. Johns, Adela Rogers: Some Are Born Great

Watson, Thomas J, and Bill Chapman: Judy: Portrait of an American Legend

Newspapers & Periodicals

The Itasca County Independent

The Los Angeles Examiner

The Los Angeles Herald

The Minneapolis Star Tribune

The NY Daily Mirror

The NY Herald Tribune

The NY Post

The Dallas Morning Star

The NY Sun

The New York Times

LOOK, LIFE, LHJ

Cosmopolitan

Redbook

The Saturday Evening Post

Good Housekeeping

Parade

Sterling Publications

Archival Material

The Margaret O'Brien Archives

The Milne Family Archives

Personal notes of Virginia Gumm Thompson

The University of The South at Sewanee

The UNL Archives of Canada

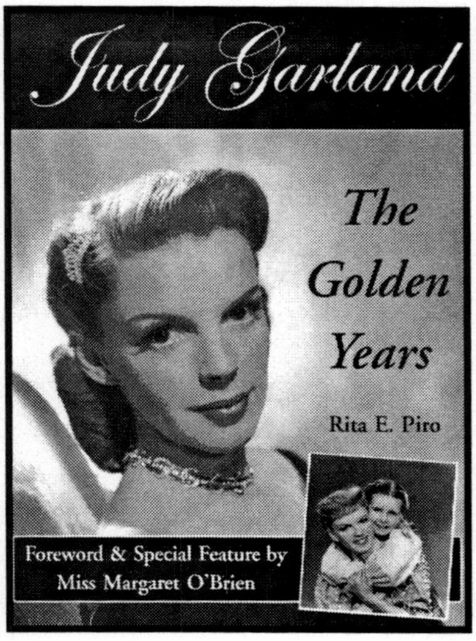